Copyright © 2023. React Ready: Learn modern React with TypeScript. Authored by Steven Spadotto. A **Lumin8 Media** publication (https://lumin8media.com)

All rights reserved. This book, or parts thereof, may n_____d in any retrieval system, or transmitted in any form by any m_____, photocopy, recording, or otherwise - without prior written permission of the author, except as provided by Canadian copyright law.

Table of Contents

Welcome to React Ready! 3

Introduction 4

JavaScript Refresher 7

Introduction to React 28

Getting started with React 34

JSX 43

Components 48

Fundamental Hooks 84

Forms 180

Custom Hooks 185

Performance Hooks 198

Styling React components 241

Context 250

What's next? 278

Welcome to React Ready!

Hello, I'm Steven Spadotto. I've been a full-stack web developer for over 10 years. I've had the pleasure to work for great companies in the education, gaming, and e-commerce industries, where I helped architecture, design, and develop web applications. Over the years, I gained valuable experience working with in-demand front-end technologies such as JavaScript, TypeScript, Angular, and of course, React.

Throughout my career, I've had the pleasure to mentor several front-end developers. It has given me the opportunity to help them gain knowledge and experience with technologies such as React. It's a rewarding process where I get to see front-end developers get more comfortable and more confident.

I've also taught React courses for beginners. Students often asked if I could point them to a dependable resource that they could refer back to for future reference. Their inquiry motivated me to author this book.

This book dives into detail on fundamental React concepts and provides several examples to reinforce your learning. This book will take you from being a React rookie to becoming an intermediate React developer. It contains everything you need to know to get started building React apps the right way. If you want to get started building modern React web applications with TypeScript, this is the book for you.

React developers are highly sought after on the job market. I am confident that your skill set and your value on the job market will skyrocket after you grasp the material from this book.

Learning something new is never easy. Remember not to be hard on yourself. Learning takes time. Celebrate every chapter that you complete. If you get stuck and something isn't immediately clear for you, take a break and return to it later. Enjoy your learning journey, as you become *React Ready*!

Introduction

A basic understanding of JavaScript will help you learn React more effectively. The next section is a JavaScript refresher. It will keep some important JavaScript concepts, used in React, fresh in your mind before we start learning React.

This book will use React with TypeScript. A basic understanding of TypeScript is helpful for going through this book, but it is not required. You will pick up TypeScript knowledge just by reading along.

TypeScript works very well with the declarative nature of React. TypeScript helps us write more robust React code because of its type-checking.

TypeScript is an open-source programming language created by Microsoft. It's actually not a standalone programming language. It's a superset of JavaScript, which means that it is essentially JavaScript, but with additional features. TypeScript adds features to JavaScript that help us write more declarative, type-safe, and maintainable code.

System Setup

The code examples covered in this book can be found in the following GitHub repository (https://github.com/stevenspads/react-ready). To run these code examples on your local computer, you'll need the following to be installed.

- Git (https://git-scm.com/downloads)
- Node.js (https://nodejs.org/en/download)
- npm (included with Node.js installation)

Run the following commands in your terminal to see if they're properly installed.

```
git --version
node --version
npm --version
```

Cloning the GitHub repository

Included with this book is an accompanying GitHub repository. It contains all the code examples covered in the book. By cloning the repository on your local machine, you'll be able to run the code examples and inspect the output.

In order to run the application that contains all the code examples from this book, enter the following commands in your terminal.

```
git clone https://github.com/stevenspads/react-ready
cd react-ready
# if you prefer using npm, run these commands:
npm install
npm run dev
# if you prefer using yarn, run these commands:
yarn
yarn dev
```

This will start a development server at http://127.0.0.1:5173, or http://localhost:5173. When the development server starts, this address will be displayed in the terminal. Click on it to open it in your web browser. If you have another application running on port 5173, consider freeing up that port by stopping the application running on it.

The code in the GitHub repository is a React app scaffolded with Vite (https://vitejs.dev). Vite is a build tool that provides a fast and smooth development experience for building modern web apps. By default, Vite's development server runs on port 5173.

Within the application, there is a folder for each section of the book. This will make it easy for you to find the example code for the section that you are currently reading.

Tools

Let's go over a list of tools that will make your journey through this book an even more enjoyable one.

Visual Studio Code

Using **Visual Studio Code** (https://code.visualstudio.com) as a code editor will help speed up React development because of its smart IntelliSense and great TypeScript support. We can get type definitions for variables just by hovering over them. I recommend downloading and installing it.

React Developer Tools

I recommend installing the free **React Developer Tools** (https://react.dev/learn/react-developer-tools) browser extension. This extension will add React debugging tools to your browser's DevTools by creating two new DevTools tabs, **Components** and **Profiler**.

- Use the **Components** tab to inspect React components that were rendered on the page, as well as the child components that they rendered. View a component's props and state, and make changes to them on the fly.

- Use the **Profiler** tab to record performance information while interacting with a React application. Hit the *record* and *stop* buttons as needed.

JavaScript Refresher

This section contains a review of modern JavaScript features that are important to know before starting with React. Take your time to go over each feature. Make sure that you have a good understanding of each feature covered before moving on to the next sections, which are dedicated to React.

Many of these features are from JavaScript *ECMAScript 2015*, also known as *ES6*. It is a fundamental version of the *ECMAScript* standard because it adds support for several modern JavaScript features.

> *ECMAScript is the standard upon which JavaScript is based, and it's often abbreviated to ES.*

Template Literals

Template literals are sometimes referred to as template strings. Consider them supercharged strings. They are useful for string interpolation, which means replacing placeholders with values in a string. Template literals also support multiline strings.

Template literals are enclosed by the backtick character instead of the double or single quotes that accompany strings.

Without placeholders

Here's an example of a template literal that is just a basic string, without any placeholders to be replaced.

```
const text = `text as a string`;
```

Here's an example of a template literal supporting a multiline string.

```
const text = `text as a string line 1
              text as a string line 2`;
```

With placeholders

Template literals can contain placeholders. Placeholders are marked by the dollar sign and curly braces. The expressions in the placeholders are concatenated with the text outside the placeholders to form a single string.

Here's an example of a template literal with a placeholder.

```javascript
const value = 10;
const message = `The value is ${value}.`;
console.log(message); // The value is 10.
```

The placeholder can also contain JavaScript operators, such as the addition operator (+), to sum numbers.

```javascript
const first = 1;
const second = 2;
const message = `The sum of ${first} and ${second} is ${first + second}.`;
console.log(message); // The sum of 1 and 2 is 3.
```

The placeholder can also contain functions.

```javascript
function sum(first, second) {
  return first + second;
}

const first = 1;
const second = 2;
const message = `Sum: ${sum(first, second)}.`;
console.log(message); // Sum: 3.
```

Shorthand properties

Whenever we have a variable that is the same name as a property of an object, we can omit that property name when constructing that object.

The following function is written without shorthand properties.

```
function getUser(id, name, avatar) {
  return {
    id: id,
    name: name,
    avatar: avatar,
  };
}
```

Shorthand properties allow us to write a simpler function by omitting the object's property names for the object being returned.

```
function getUser(id, name, avatar) {
  return {
    id,
    name,
    avatar,
  };
}
```

The result is the same as if we did not use shorthand properties. However, shorthand properties make our code quicker to write and less verbose to read.

Let and const

Before *ES6* arrived, we were declaring variables with `var`. Code that uses variables declared with `var` is more error prone. This is why *ES6* introduced two new ways to declare variables, `let` and `const`.

Variables declared with `var` can be re-declared and updated without producing an error. This can make `var` messy to work with. If we don't realize that a variable has already been defined with `var`, and we re-define it, we can encounter unexpected results when our code runs.

Another problem with `var` is that when it declares a variable outside of a function, its scope is global. Global scope is bad for variables.

Let

`let` is meant for variables that we want to re-assign a value to. We *let* that variable be re-assignable.

```
let total = 0;

[{ total: 1 }, { total: 2 }].forEach((item) => {
  total += item.total; // reassign a new value to 'total'
});

console.log(total); // 3
```

Const

`const` stands for *constant*. It's just like `let`, but it is *immutable*, meaning that the value of a `const` can't be changed by re-assigning a new value to it. A `const` variable cannot be re-declared, and it must be assigned a value when it is declared.

```
const favoriteNumber = 5;

// Uncaught TypeError: Assignment to constant variable.
favoriteNumber = 10;
```

If a `const` variable is an *object* or an *array*, its properties, or items, are allowed to be updated. Consider the following object initialized with `const`.

```
const user = {
  name: "John",
};
user.age = 20;
console.log(user); // { name: "John", age: 20 }
```

Even though the `user` object is declared with `const`, we can assign new properties to the object or modify the values of existing ones. `const` does not prevent objects from being modified, it only prevents the variable itself from being reassigned.

```
const user = {
  name: "John",
};

// Uncaught TypeError: Assignment to constant variable.
user = { name: "Smith" };
```

Consider the following array initialized with `const`.

```
const numbers = [1,2,3];
numbers.push(4);
console.log(numbers); // [1,2,3,4]
```

Even though the numbers array is declared with const, we are able to update the variable. In this case, we added a number to it.

In modern JavaScript code, you'll see no var declarations, just let and const. The const declaration is the most widely used because of how important immutability is.

We should always declare a variable with const unless we know that the value will change over time.

Scope

The let and const variable declarations are block-scoped, which means that the variables exist only within the corresponding block. Whenever you see curly brackets, {...}, it is the definition of a block. This means you can define the same variable name in different scopes/blocks and not encounter an error for doing so.

```
let car = "Ferrari";

if (car) {
  let car = "Mitsubishi";
  console.log(car); // Mitsubishi
}

console.log(car); // Ferrari
```

There is no error produced by the code above. Both instances of the car variable are seen as different variables because they have different scopes.

Arrow functions

Arrow functions are a compact alternative to traditional functions. They work the same way that traditional functions do, but they have a different syntax.

```
// traditional function
function add(a, b) {
  return a + b;
}

// arrow function (implicit return)
const add = (a, b) => a + b;

// arrow function (explicit return)
const add = (a, b) => {
  return a + b;
};
```

Combining `const` and arrow functions has become quite popular. Many developers find the traditional function syntax to be more verbose.

There is one important difference between arrow functions and traditional functions That difference is related to *hoisting*.

Hoisting is something that JavaScript does during its compile phase, just microseconds before code is executed. Code is scanned for function and variable declarations. All functions and variable declarations are added to memory inside a JavaScript data structure. This allows them to be used even before they are actually declared in the code.

```
helloWorld();
// prints 'Hello World' to the console

function helloWorld() {
  console.log("Hello World");
}
```

In this example, the `helloWorld` function is called even before it is actually declared.

The same is not true for arrow functions. Using an uninitialized `const` variable before it is declared results in a syntax error.

```
greeting("John");

const greeting = (text) => {
  console.log(text);
};
```

This code will throw an error because the `greeting` arrow function is called before it is declared. To fix the error, we must declare the arrow function before it is called.

```
const greeting = (text) => {
  console.log(text);
};

greeting("John");
```

If we want to keep our functions at the bottom of a file and use them before they are declared, we should use the traditional function syntax. This will allow the functions to be hoisted to the top of the file.

Destructuring

JavaScript array and object destructuring allows us to break up arrays and objects into their individual pieces. Arrays and objects are the two most used data structures in JavaScript. Therefore, it's important to know how to destructure them.

Array destructuring

Here is an example of a function that destructures an array into variables.

```
function printName(fullName) {
  const [firstName, lastName] = fullName;
  console.log(firstName); // John
  console.log(lastName);  // Smith
}

printName(["John", "Smith"]);
```

The destructuring assignment does not modify the original array. It just copies the array items into dedicated variables.

Without array destructuring, we would have to write code that is more verbose. Let's take a look at what that would look like.

```
function printName(fullName) {
  const firstName = fullName[0];
  const lastName = fullName[1];
  console.log(firstName); // John
  console.log(lastName); // Smith
}

printName(["John", "Smith"]);
```

We have the option to skip over array elements while destructuring.

```
const [firstName, , title] = ["John", "Smith", "President"];

console.log(firstName); // John
console.log(title); // President
```

We can also use object properties for the left-hand side of the destructuring syntax.

```
const person = {};
[person.firstName, person.lastName] = "John Smith".split(" ");
console.log(person.firstName); // John
console.log(person.lastName); // Smith
```

The `split` function broke up the string wherever a space was found. Since there was only one space between "John" and "Smith", the string was broken up into an array of two elements containing "John" and "Smith".

We can set a default value for any missing elements during destructuring.

```
const [firstName, lastName, title = "No Title"] = ["John", "Smith"];
console.log(firstName); // John
console.log(lastName); // Smith
console.log(title); // No Title
```

We can use the JavaScript *spread* syntax to get the remaining values of an array while destructuring.

```
const [firstName, middleName, ...data] = [
  "John",
  "James",
  "Smith",
  "President",
];

console.log(firstName); // John
console.log(middleName); // James
console.log(Array.isArray(data)); // true
```

```
console.log(data.length); // 2
console.log(data[0]); // Smith
console.log(data[1]); // President
```

Object destructuring

The destructuring assignment doesn't only work with arrays, it also works with objects. On the right side of the destructuring assignment is an existing object. On the left side of the destructuring assignment are the properties that we want to extract from that object.

```
const user = {
  firstName: "John",
  lastName: "Smith",
  age: 20,
};

const { firstName, lastName } = user;

console.log(firstName); // John
console.log(lastName); // Smith
```

If we want to assign a property to a variable with a name other than the name of the object property, we can set a new name using the colon operator.

```
const user = {
  firstName: "John",
  lastName: "Smith",
  age: 20,
};

const { firstName: first, lastName: last, age } = user;

console.log(first); // John
console.log(last); // Smith
console.log(age); // 20
```

The colon operator tells us what value goes where. In this example, it allows the value for the user object property, `firstName`, to go into a variable named `first`.

If an object has more properties than we need variables, then we can assign the rest of the properties using the *spread* syntax. This is similar to what we did when destructuring arrays.

```
const user = {
  firstName: "John",
  lastName: "Smith",
  age: 20,
```

```
};

const { firstName, ...data } = user;

console.log(firstName); // John
console.log(data.lastName); // Smith
console.log(data.age); // 20
```

Parameter defaults

Default function parameters allow function parameters to be initialized with default values if no value is passed, or if a value of undefined is passed.

```
function add(a, b = 0) {
  return a + b;
}

console.log(add(1, 2)); // 3
console.log(add(1)); // 1
```

Default function parameters allow us to save on the code that we would usually write to check function parameters for a value of undefined.

Without default function parameters, we would traditionally write something like the following.

```
function add(a, b) {
  return a + (b === undefined ? 0 : b);
}

console.log(add(1, 2)); // 3
console.log(add(1, undefined)); // 1
```

Rest/Spread operator

Rest syntax resembles spread syntax. They both use .... However, rest syntax actually behaves the opposite of spread syntax. Rest syntax collects multiple elements and condenses them into a single element. Instead, spread syntax expands, or opens up, an array or object into its elements.

Rest

Rest syntax can be used to allow a function to accept any number of arguments as an array.

```
function sum(...args) {
  return args.reduce((previous, current) => {
```

```
    return previous + current;
  });
}

console.log(sum(1, 2, 3)); // 6
```

Spread

Spread syntax can be used when all the elements of an object or array need to be included somewhere.

```
function add(a, b, c) {
  return a + b + c;
}

const numbers = [1, 2, 3];

console.log(add(...numbers)); // 6
```

Spread syntax is most commonly used when combining items.

```
const numbers = [1, 2, 3];
const newNumber = 4;
const allNumbers = [...numbers, newNumber]; // [1, 2, 3, 4]
```

Spread syntax is also commonly used to combine objects.

```
const user = {
  firstName: "John",
  lastName: "John",
};

const userDetails = {
  age: 20,
};

const profile = { ...user, ...userDetails };
console.log(profile); // { age: 20, firstName: 'John', LastName: 'Smith' }
```

The spread operator is less verbose than using the `Object.assign` method, which does the same thing.

```
const user = {
  firstName: "John",
  lastName: "John",
};
```

```
const userDetails = {
  age: 20,
};

const profile = Object.assign({}, user, userDetails);
console.log(profile); // { age: 20, firstName: 'John', LastName: 'Smith' }
```

Ternary operator

The ternary operator allows us to write shorter `if/else` statements. We can take traditional `if/else` code blocks, like the one below, and apply the ternary operator.

```
let user;
if (user) {
  message = "User found";
} else {
  message = "User not found";
}

console.log(message); // "User not found"
```

Here is the same condition written using the ternary operator.

```
let user;
const message = user ? "User found" : "User not found";

console.log(message); // "User not found"
```

Optional chaining

The optional chaining operator, `?.`, is for optional property access. Optional chaining allows us to write code that will immediately stop running some expressions if a `null` or `undefined` value is found.

Consider the following example demonstrating object property access on an `undefined` object.

```
let user;
const name = user.firstName;

// TypeError: Cannot read properties of undefined (reading 'firstName')
```

This code will throw an error. The `user` object is `undefined` because we never initialized it. Thus, no properties can be accessed from the `user` object. The optional chaining operator helps us to avoid this error during object property access.

```
let user;
const name = user?.firstName;
console.log(name); // undefined
```

After applying optional chaining to the code above, it no longer throws an error. Instead, it logs `undefined` to the console.

We can also use optional chaining for nested object properties.

```
const user = {};
const zip = user?.address?.zip;
console.log(zip); // undefined
```

Before optional chaining came along, we had to write long expressions, such as the one below, in order to avoid accessing a property on an `undefined` variable.

```
const user = {};
const zip = user && user.address && user.address.zip;
console.log(zip); // undefined
```

Optional chaining for arrays

Optional chaining can also be used on arrays.

```
const array = ["John"];
const item = array?.[1];
console.log(item); // undefined
```

This code will run without producing an error, even if there is no array element at position 1. When no element is found at the referenced array position, `undefined` is returned.

Optional chaining for functions

We can also use optional chaining on functions.

```
const user = {
  name: "John",
};
console.log(user.sendEmail?.()); // undefined
```

This code will run without producing an error, even if the `sendEmail` function was never defined on the `user` object.

Nullish coalescing operator

The nullish coalescing operator, ??, will return the operand on its right-hand side when its operand on the left-hand side is null or undefined. Otherwise, it will return the operand on the left-hand side.

Here's how we wrote code before the nullish coalescing operator came along.

```
const total = null || 100;
console.log(total); // 100
```

We can re-write this using the nullish coalescing operator.

```
const total = null ?? 100;
console.log(total); // 100
```

Array methods

Let's go over some of the most helpful JavaScript array methods. These array methods are commonly used in React.

find()

```
const numbers = [5, 12, 2, 20, 40];
const found = numbers.find((number) => number > 10);
console.log(found); // 12
```

The find method will return the first element in the array that satisfies the condition supplied in the testing function that find uses internally. The array is not modified.

some()

```
const numbers = [1, 2, 3];
const result = numbers.some((number) => number > 1);
console.log(result); // true
```

The some method checks if at least one element in the array passes the test implemented by the function supplied to some. A value of true will be returned if an element in the array passes the test supplied by the provided function. The test performed is simply a conditional expression. The array is not modified.

every()

```
const numbers = [10, 20, 30];
const result = numbers.every((number) => number < 40);
console.log(result); // true
```

The every method checks if all elements in an array pass the test implemented by the function supplied to every. If all elements pass the test, `true` is returned. If not, `false` is returned. The array is not modified.

includes()

```
const fruits = ["apple", "banana", "peach"];
console.log(fruits.includes("apple")); // true
console.log(fruits.includes("mango")); // false
```

The includes method checks if an array includes a value in any of its items. It returns `true` if the array includes that value, and `false` otherwise. The array is not modified.

map()

```
const numbers = [1, 2, 3];
const result = numbers.map((number) => number * 2);
console.log(result); // [2, 4, 6]
```

The map method creates a new array. The new array contains the result of calling the function supplied to map on every item in the original array. The map method will return an empty array if the source array has no items in it.

filter()

```
const words = ["test", "code", "editor", "react"];
const result = words.filter((word) => word.length > 4);
console.log(result); // ["editor", "react"]
```

The filter method creates a new array with all the elements that pass the test implemented by the function supplied to filter. The array is not modified.

reduce()

The reduce method is one of the more challenging JavaScript methods to understand. Like its name implies, reduce allows us to reduce an array using a *reducer* function. The reducer function performs an accumulation of an array's values in order to reduce that array to a single result.

```
const numbers = [1, 2, 3];
const sum = numbers.reduce((sum, number) => {
  console.log(sum); // 0, then 1, then 3, then 6
  return sum + number;
}, 0);
console.log(sum); // 6
```

In this example, an array of numbers gets reduced to a sum of 6. The arrow function within reduce is a callback function that gets invoked for every item in the array. The second argument passed to reduce is 0. This initializes the accumulator with an initial value.

The sum variable is the accumulator. The accumulator collects the function's accumulated result. It starts with the initial value of 0. The return value of each iteration is used as the new accumulator value for the next iteration.

For the first iteration, sum is 1 (0 + 1). For the second iteration, sum is 3 (1 + 2). For the third iteration, sum is 6 (3 + 3).

The reduce method will not change the original array. The reduce method will not run if the array has no items.

Async and await

The `async` and `await` keywords reduce the boilerplate code that is usually need for promises in JavaScript. Promises are objects that represent the eventual completion or failure of an asynchronous operation, and the resulting value of that operation.

The `async` and `await` keywords make asynchronous code look like it's synchronous. Let's take a look at an example.

```
const getUsers = () => {
  return new Promise((resolve) => {
    setTimeout(() => resolve(["John", "Jane"]), 3000);
  });
};

const printUsers = async () => {
  const users = await getUsers();
  console.log(users);
};

console.log("Before...");
printUsers();
console.log("After...");
```

The `getUsers` function implements a timer with a delay of 3 seconds to simulate an asynchronous operation. It then returns a promise.

To call the `getUsers` function from another function, we need to define the calling function using the `async` keyword. Then, when we make the call to `getUsers`, we must prepend `await` before it. This will make the call stop until the promise is resolved or rejected.

The above example will log the following to the browser console.

```
"Before...";
"After..."[("John", "Jane")]; //after 3 seconds
```

Prepending the `async` keyword to any function will make it return a promise. Even if the function does not explicitly do so, `async` will make it return a promise.

Code that uses `async` and `await` looks much simpler compared to traditional asynchronous JavaScript code that uses promise chaining with the `then` method and callback functions. Using `async` and `await` make asynchronous JavaScript code simpler to read, code, test, and debug.

ES Modules

A module is a JavaScript file that exports one or more objects, functions, or variables, using the `export` keyword.

The syntax to import a module is the following.

```
import item from "module";
```

One or more exports

We can export one or more variables from a module. Remember, a module is just a JavaScript file that exports objects, functions, or variables. Let's call this file `module.js`.

```
const one = 1;
const two = 2;
const three = 3;

export { one, two, three };
```

Another JavaScript file or module can import all the exports from `module.js`. Let's assume this other file is in the same folder as `module.js`. Here's how we can import all of the `module.js` exports in another file.

```
import * from './module.js';
```

We can also import just a select few of the exports rather than all of them. We will use the object destructuring syntax for this.

```
import { one } from "./module.js";
```

We can rename any import, for convenience, or to fix variable name clashes, using the `as` keyword.

```
import { one, two as second } from "./module.js";
```

Default export

Default exports are useful when we want to export only a single object, function, variable from a module. In this case, a module will define a single *default* export.

We can create a default export using the `default` keyword. Let's create a file named `slugify.js`. In it, we'll define a function that will convert any string that we send it to lowercase.

```
export default function slugify(input) {
  return input.toLowerCase();
}
```

We can also write the default export on a separate line.

```
function slugify(input) {
  return input.toLowerCase();
}

export default slugify;
```

Since `default` defines a single export, the `slugify` function could also be defined as an anonymous function that we do not have to name.

```
export default (input) => input.toLowerCase();
```

Any JavaScript file can then import the function provided by the `slugify.js` module. When we import a `default` export, we can use any name we want.

```
import toSlug from "./slugify.js";

toSlug("Testing"); // testing
```

When importing default exports, they do not need curly brackets around the imported name like the non-default exports do.

It's also possible to import a `default` export and a non-default export at the same time. Let's define a `strings.js` module that has both a `default` and non-default export.

```
export default (input) => input.toLowerCase();

const toUpperCase = (input) => input.toUpperCase();
```

```
export { toUpperCase };
```

Now, let's import both exports from `strings.js` in another JavaScript file.

```
import toLowerCase, { toUpperCase } from "./strings.js";

console.log(toLowerCase("John")); // john
console.log(toUpperCase("John")); // JOHN
```

We imported the `default` export using a name that we were free to pick, `toLowerCase`. We were forced to import the non-default export of `toUpperCase` using the name it was defined with.

Recap

We've reached the end of the JavaScript refresher. I hope this section helped you get up to speed with modern JavaScript. You should now be feeling more confident to jump into React in the next chapter!

Introduction to React

React is a JavaScript library for building front-end user interfaces. React aims to make it simple to create user-interfaces (UIs) that are both fast and interactive. React allows developers to build complex UIs from small and separate pieces of code that exist in isolation, called components.

In this section, we will cover the following:

- Why learn React?
- Why is React so popular?
- The advantages of React.

Why learn React?

Are there good reasons for learning React today? There sure are! Let's take a look at the best reasons for learning React.

- React's APIs are not very large, they are not too difficult to learn, and they do not change often.

- The React community is very large, which means there are plenty of learning resources online.

- React has a large ecosystem of free tools, hooks, and components.

- React developers are highly sought after in the job market.

- React is backed by very large companies.

Even if React was released in 2013, it's never been too late to learn it. It's adoption rate and popularity keeps on growing, even after all these years. React doesn't look it will be going away anytime soon.

Why is React so popular?

Since it's inception, React has quickly become the library of choice for building dynamic user-interfaces. Let's look at some reasons why React has become so popular.

- React was the first front-end library to introduce a component-based architecture.

- React is declarative.

- React allows for fast DOM (Document Object Model) updates thanks to its Virtual DOM (VDOM).

- React can be used for making both web and mobile applications. React Native is used for mobile app development and is derived from React.

- React is used by companies of all sizes. Notable companies are: Facebook, Instagram, WhatsApp, New York Times, Netflix, Airbnb, Discord, etc.

- React has a huge developer community, providing many online resources and tools to help React developers.

The advantages of React

Let's take an in-depth look at the following advantages of React:

- React is declarative.
- React uses a virtual DOM.
- React is functional.
- React is component-based.

React is declarative

What does *declarative* even mean, right? The term comes from *Declarative Programming*, which consists of telling the computer what needs to be done, rather than describing exactly how to do it.

React makes it easy to express what our web application will look like, without having to worry about manually updating the DOM.

> *DOM is an acronym that stands for Document Object Model. Web browsers use this model to create an internal representation of a web page. The DOM is responsible for determining what elements should be on a page and how those elements relate to the other elements on the page.*

React takes care of modifying the DOM for us so that we can focus on building our user-interface. With React, we simply describe what we want to see on the screen and React takes care of the rest. We don't need to specify every single DOM modification required to display our user-interface. React allows us to build web pages without ever directly manipulating the DOM.

When the state of our application changes, React figures out which parts of our application need to be updated, and will render these updates to the screen. When it comes to rendering updates to the screen, React will use the least number of DOM mutations possible to keep DOM updates fast.

In the past, when we needed to update what was displayed on the screen, vanilla JavaScript and *JQuery* both forced us to code a series of steps to manually update the DOM. With React, we can simply change a component's state, and that component will be automatically updated on the screen according to its current state.

React makes it easy for us to know what a component will look like once it is displayed on the screen. All we have to do is look at the code and markup tags that are included in the return statement of a component.

React uses a virtual DOM

React uses a virtual DOM (VDOM). Why does React use a virtual DOM, you ask? While modern JavaScript performance keeps improving, reading from and writing to the DOM remains slow.

Modern websites and web apps can end up performing large amounts of DOM manipulations, many of which are not even necessary. Inefficiently updating the DOM can become a very serious problem for websites and web apps. In order to solve this issue and bypass the slowness of the DOM, React created the virtual DOM.

React keeps a lightweight virtual representation of the DOM in memory, called virtual DOM. Manipulating the virtual DOM is much faster than manipulating the actual DOM, because nothing gets drawn on the screen when the virtual DOM is manipulated. Manipulating the virtual DOM is like editing the blueprints of a vehicle's design rather than making changes to an actual vehicle.

For every DOM object on the screen, React creates a corresponding virtual DOM object. The virtual DOM object is similar to a lightweight copy of the actual DOM object.

When there is a change in the data of a component, React will produces an update to the virtual DOM. A new virtual representation of the DOM is created. React will then compare the new virtual DOM with a virtual DOM snapshot that was taken right before the update took place. React does this comparison in order to find out which virtual DOM objects changed. This process is known as *diffing* because React is looking for *differences* between snapshots.

The *diffing* process allows React to know exactly which virtual DOM objects have changed. Once React knows what changed, React will update *only* the objects that changed in the real DOM. When updating the real DOM, React computes the minimal set of changes that are required to update it, and then patches those changes to the real DOM. Changes appear on the screen only when the real DOM is updated.

Let's say we have a React website that displays a list of items. When a user selects the first item in the list, React won't rebuild the entire list. React will only rebuild the list item whose state changed from a deselected state to a selected state. The selected list item is rebuilt in the DOM in order to display its new state. The rest of the list items will remain untouched in the DOM because their state did not change.

The innovation of the virtual DOM is why React is known for being such a performant library.

Elements in React's Virtual DOM

React's virtual DOM implements a browser-independent DOM system for performance reasons and for improving cross-browser compatibility. React's DOM system has a few differences compared to the browser DOM that we are used to. In React, all DOM properties, attributes, and event handlers must be *camelCased*.

DOM property changes

Here are some examples of DOM properties that must be camelCased in React.

- `tabindex` becomes `tabIndex`
- `readonly` becomes `readOnly`
- `onclick` becomes `onClick`

DOM attribute changes

Here are some examples of DOM attributes that must be camelCased in React.

- `class` becomes `className` to add CSS classes to elements.

- `for` becomes `htmlFor`, since `for` is a reserved word in JavaScript.

- `selected` is not used for `<option>` tags. To mark one as selected, reference its value using `<select value={2}>`. This will mark `<option value={2}>2</option>` as selected within the select box.

- `style` accepts a JavaScript object with camelCased properties rather than a CSS string. Using it to style elements is not recommended. Use `className` instead.

The exceptions to the camelCased rule are `aria-*` and `data-*` attributes, which remain lowercase.

React is functional

React components are just JavaScript functions. React implements components as pure JavaScript functions. Pure functions belong to the *functional programming* paradigm.

> *Given the same inputs, a pure function will always return the same value, regardless of how many times the function is called. Also, a pure function does not modify any data outside of its scope.*

React components are defined by *props*, which are external parameters, and *state*, which is internal component data. Given the same props and state, a React component will render the same view on the screen. This is how React implements the concept of pure functions in its design.

Since React components are pure functions, we can reuse components in different parts of our web application without wondering what to expect. The purity of React components makes them predictable. We know that components will always behave the same way given the same props and state.

React is component-based

React's component-based architecture provides the following advantages.

- **Reusability:** Building a user-interface with the component-based approach makes it very easy to reuse components and avoid code duplication.

- **Self-documented:** The *props* (external parameters) that are defined by a React component make that component self-documented. Every developer who uses that component knows what is needed to use it.

- **Encapsulation:** Components are isolated units. The logic and presentation that a component encapsulates should not affect other components or be affected by other components. This makes it simple to move components around without surprises.

Recap

Now that we've learned what React is and why it's so great, let's start building with it in the next section.

Getting started with React

In this section, we'll learn about React elements, the building blocks of every React application. We'll see how to add React to a traditional web page. Then, we'll look at React project development tools that will take our developer experience to the next level when building React applications.

React elements

Elements are the smallest building blocks of React applications. They are not to be confused with React components. React components are made up of one or many React elements.

A React element is a virtual representation of a DOM element. React elements live in React's virtual DOM (VDOM). Compared to manipulating actual DOM nodes, React can create and destroy its elements in a very performant way.

A React element is a plain JavaScript object describing a React component or a HTML tag and its attributes. A React element is a way of telling React what we want to see on the screen. A React element contains the following:

- **type**: the type of the element. It can be a string for HTML tags or a reference to a React component.

- **props**: an object containing the element's properties, or props.

- **children:** the children of the element. It can be a string or an array of child elements.

Let's take a look at a simple React element.

```
const h1Element = <h1 className="SomeClass">Hello, world!</h1>;
```

The object representation of this React element would look like the following.

```
{
  type: 'h1',
  props: {
    className: 'SomeClass',
    children: 'Hello, world!'
  }
}
```

34

The definition of h1Element above created an object with a 'h1' type, and with props className and children. The children prop contains the a string representing the text that was passed in between the opening and closing <h1> tags, and the className contains the string that was passed to it.

A React element can be created in two different ways.

1. Using createElement.
2. Using *JSX*.

Creating elements with createElement()

```
import { createElement } from "react";
const h1Element = createElement("h1", null, "Hello, World");
```

The example above creates a React element using the createElement method provided by React.

The first argument passed to createElement specifies the type of element to create. In this case, it's a h1 HTML tag. It could have also been a custom React component. When creating a HTML element, we pass in the type as a string, as we did above. When creating a React component, we pass in the component name as the type.

The second argument for createElement is an object containing properties (*props* in React) for the element. In this case, we added no properties to our h1 element.

The last argument for createElement is its children. This can be a string. The string gets interpreted as text. However, we can also use this argument to pass in a reference to another element, allowing for element nesting.

If we want to apply CSS styling to our element, we can do so by providing a property called className.

```
import { createElement } from "react";
const element = createElement("h1", { className: "title" }, "Hello, World");
```

If we want to apply element nesting, we can do the following.

```
import { createElement } from "react";

const title = createElement("h1", null, "Hello, World");
```

```
const paragraph = createElement("p", null, "Paragraph");
const container = createElement("div", null, [title, paragraph]);
```

After creating React elements with the `createElement` method, they can then be rendered to a web page using the `render` method. More on this later.

Creating elements with JSX

The very first example of a React element that we saw above used JSX to create a React element.

```
const element = <h1>Hello, world</h1>;
```

React elements created with JSX are transpiled to `createElement` functions in order to create React elements that will represent the application's user-interface.

Both approaches achieve the same result, but using JSX is quicker, requires less code, and is more readable when there's more elements involved.

Adding React to a web page

When a user visits a web page, the server will return an `index.html` file to the browser that might look something like this.

```
<html>
  <body>
    <div>
      <h1>Welcome</h1>
      <p>This is a page.</p>
    </div>
  </body>
</html>
```

The web browser will read the HTML file that it received and use it to construct the DOM (Document Object Model). The DOM for the HTML file above would look something like this.

```
HTML
 |
BODY
 |
DIV
|  |
H1 P
```

The DOM has a tree-like structure, containing parent and child relationships. The browser uses the hierarchy of HTML tags on the page that it loads to build this tree-like structure.

The DOM is important for us programmers because it is what lives between our code and the user interface. If we want our code to actually show something on a web page, that code must make use of the DOM.

The DOM provides us with methods that we can use via a programming language like JavaScript in order to manipulate the DOM tree or listen to user events. We can manipulate the DOM by adding, updating, or deleting elements from the tree.

React setup

To use React on a basic web page, we can load the necessary React scripts from an external website that provides them. This is the quickest way to start using React.

Let's load React scripts from an external website called unpkg.com. The following two scripts are required for using React on a web page.

- **react**: The core React library.
- **react-dom**: A script that gives us DOM-specific methods so that we can use React with the DOM.

Let's add these scripts at the bottom of the body section in our `index.html` file. We'll also take this opportunity to remove the content that was previously in that file.

```
<html>
  <body>
    <script src="https://unpkg.com/react@18.2.0/umd/react.development.js"></script>
    <script src="https://unpkg.com/react-dom@18.2.0/umd/react-dom.development.js"></script>
  </body>
</html>
```

We specified `18.2.0` as the React version for these scripts. At the time of the writing of this book, it's the most recent React version available.

Now, let's add a container HTML element for our React application. We'll use a `<div>` tag and give it an `id` of app. We could have given it any unique identifier. Everything that will be inside this HTML element will be managed by React's virtual DOM rather than by the browser DOM.

```
<html>
  <body>
    <div id="app"></div>
    <script src="https://unpkg.com/react@17/umd/react.development.js"></script>
    <script src="https://unpkg.com/react-dom@17/umd/react-dom.development.js"></script>
  </body>
</html>
```

The `<div id="app">` element that we added is referred to as a *root* DOM node. React applications usually have just a single root node.

We're now ready to reference the root node so that we can render React elements in it.

```
<html>
  <body>
    <div id="app"></div>

    <script
```

```
    src="https://unpkg.com/react@17/umd/react.development.js"></script>
    <script src="https://unpkg.com/react-dom@17/umd/react-dom.development.js"></script>
    <script type="text/javascript">
      const app = document.getElementById('app'); ReactDOM.render(
      <h1>Hello World</h1>, app);
    </script>
  </body>
</html>
```

We added a `<script type="text/javascript">` tag to contain the logic for rendering React elements in the root node. We used the `getElementById` DOM method to reference the root note that we created. Then, we used the `ReactDOM.render` method from the `react-dom` script to tell React that we want to render a React element that we created with JSX inside of the root node.

If we now try running this code in our web browser, we will get a JavaScript error in the console of our browser. If you are using the Google Chrome web browser, you can open your browser console to view the error using *Command + Option + J* on Mac, or *Control + Shift + J* on Windows.

```
Uncaught SyntaxError: Unexpected token '<'
```

This error occurred because the `<h1>Hello World</h1>` element that we told React to render inside the root node is actually not valid JavaScript. The `<h1>Hello World</h1>` code is not JavaScript code, it's JSX code.

JSX is a syntax extension for JavaScript that allows us to code our user interface using a HTML-like syntax. If we know HTML and JavaScript, there is no new syntax for us to learn to use JSX. We just need to learn a few JSX rules and then practice using it. There will be more on JSX in an upcoming section dedicated to it.

Web browsers don't understand JSX. We will need to include *Babel*. Babel is a JavaScript compiler that will transform our JSX code into regular JavaScript code.

Adding Babel

To include Babel on our web page, let's add the Babel script to our `index.html` file. Let's also change our script type from `text/javascript` to `text/jsx`. This will indicate that our script contains JSX code.

```
<html>
  <body>
```

```
    <div id="app"></div>

    <script
src="https://unpkg.com/react@17/umd/react.development.js"></script>
    <script src="https://unpkg.com/react-dom@17/umd/react-
dom.development.js"></script>
    <script src="https://unpkg.com/@babel/standalone/babel.min.js"></script>
    <script type="text/jsx">
      const app = document.getElementById('app'); ReactDOM.render(
      <h1>Hello World</h1>, app);
    </script>
  </body>
</html>
```

Now, if we run this `index.html` file in our web browser, we will see `Hello World` displayed on the web page within h1 tags.

React project development tools

Using React the way we've used it until now can work fine. However, since there are much better React project development tools available to us today, we may not want to be developing an entire React web application like this. Let's consider these tools and improve our developer experience.

Vite

Vite (https://vitejs.dev) is a very performant front-end tool that gives us a development server to run our React application locally, and a *build* command that bundles our code, producing optimized static assets for production.

Vite supports modern front-end libraries such as React, Vue, Preact, and Svelte, and it has TypeScript support.

To create a Vite-powered React application with TypeScript support, called `myapp`, enter the following command in your terminal.

```
npm init vite@latest myapp -- --template react-ts
```

You will be prompted with the following.

```
Need to install the following packages:
  create-vite@4.2.0
Ok to proceed? (y)
```

Simply type y to accept. Vite will then scaffold your project.

```
Done. Now run:
cd myapp
npm install
npm run dev
```

Once it's done, run the provided commands to switch to the new `myapp` project folder, install all dependencies, and run the development server. Congratulations! You've just used Vite to create a fresh new React project with TypeScript support.

React strict mode

Vite enables React *strict mode* by default. You'll notice `StrictMode` tags wrapping the app in the project's `main.tsx` file. With strict mode enabled, React will intentionally run some lifecycle methods twice to help detect errors. This only applies to development mode. Lifecycle methods will not be double-invoked in production mode.

The reason why React's strict mode runs some lifecycle methods twice is because it assumes that every component we create is a *pure function*. As pure functions, React components must always return the same JSX given the same inputs (props, state, and context).

Components that break the pure function rule will end up behaving unpredictably and become a source for bugs. To help us find impure code, React's strict mode will call some of our functions twice in development.

The functions called twice in development are those that should be pure. They are:

- Code in the component body (but not event handler functions).

- Functions that are passed to the `useState`, `useMemo`, or `useReducer` Hooks.

- State setter functions for the `useState` Hook.

Don't worry if none of these React Hooks are familiar to you yet. You'll learn all about them in upcoming sections of this book.

Keep React strict mode in mind when running the code examples provided throughout this book. There will be some examples where duplicate messages will be logged to the console twice. It's not a problem with the code. It's just React strict mode doing its thing.

React frameworks

React applications built with Vite are rendered in the web browser. This is referred to as *client-side rendering* (CSR). With client-side rendering, the browser gets a web page but sees no HTML at first. The browser must execute the JavaScript code on the web page in order to build the DOM and make the web page visible. JavaScript must be enabled in the user's browser for the application to load properly.

Next.js (https://nextjs.org) and **Remix** (https://remix.run) are two popular React frameworks that take advantage of *server-side rendering* (SSR). With server-side rendering, the server's response to the web browser contains all the HTML of a web page already loaded and ready to be displayed.

Depending on the type of application, server-side rendering can have several advantages over client-side rendering. However, if you are just starting off with React, I recommend using Vite before trying SSR frameworks.

This book and it's accompanying GitHub repository (https://github.com/stevenspads/react-ready) use Vite to build a React application.

JSX

Google's Angular framework separates markup and logic in separate files, putting markup in a HTML file, and logic in a TypeScript file. React takes a different approach. React components contain both markup and logic. With React, component logic is combined with user interface logic in the same file.

While some might argue that this is not a proper separation of concerns, React sees it differently. React chooses to separate concerns using *loosely coupled* components that contain both markup and logic. The way that React components can contain both markup and logic is via JSX.

What is JSX?

JSX, which stands for JavaScript XML, is an extension to JavaScript syntax. It allows HTML-like code to be written within JavaScript code, and it allows JavaScript code to be written within HTML-like code. Take a look at the following line of code.

```
const element = <h1>Hello, world!</h1>;
```

What kind of code is this? Is it JavaScript? Is it HTML? Or, is it something else? It almost seems like JavaScript code, since it starts with `const`. However, if we try to run this code in a JavaScript file, it won't work. The code also contains a `<h1>` tag, which looks exactly like HTML. However, if we try to run this code in a HTML file, it won't work.

This syntax is not JavaScript or HTML. It's called *JSX*. It looks like a template language, but it actually has all the power of JavaScript. The example above consists of a basic unit of JSX.

JSX was written to be used with React. JSX is very helpful to know because we can use it to produce React elements, which we covered in detail in the previous section.

JSX expressions are interpreted as JavaScript expressions, which means that they can go anywhere that JavaScript expressions can go. We can assign a JSX expression to a variable, pass a JSX expression to a function, store a JSX expression in an object or an array, and more.

JSX is a syntax extension to JavaScript, which means that JSX itself is not valid JavaScript. Web browsers do not understand JSX. JSX needs to be compiled to be understood by web browsers. JSX expressions get compiled to plain JavaScript code after the compilation step of a React application. Thanks to compilation, we can use JSX within JavaScript code, and we can use JavaScript code within JSX code.

React does not force us to use JSX. Anything we can do with JSX, we can also do with JavaScript. However, JSX makes it quicker and easier to develop React components. Most developers like JSX because it allows them to build their user interface directly from JavaScript code. Developers also like JSX because it provides useful warnings and error messages.

React component files that contain JSX must be saved with a `.jsx` extension, or a `.tsx` extension if TypeScript is used.

Using JSX

Variables in JSX

We can use JavaScript variables in JSX by wrapping them in curly braces.

```
const name = "John Smith";
const element = <h1>Hello, {name}</h1>;
```

HTML attributes in JSX

JSX allows us to use curly braces to embed a JavaScript expression in a HTML attribute.

```
const element = <img src={user.imageUrl} />;
```

JavaScript expressions in JSX

Any valid JavaScript expression can go inside the curly braces in JSX. When we say JavaScript expression, we are referring to any valid code that resolves to a value.

```
const element = <h1>Hello, {2 + 2}</h1>;
```

When the `element` is rendered to the DOM, the embedded JavaScript expression is evaluated to be 4. This example produces a h1 tag with the text, "Hello, 4."

Empty HTML elements in JSX

In JSX, we must explicitly close empty HTML elements. Empty HTML elements are elements that have no closing tag. We explicitly close them using a closing slash at the end of their tag.

- `<br>` must be `<br />`
- `<img>` must be `<img />`
- `<input>` must be `<input />`

Nesting in JSX

With JSX, we can nest elements within other elements, just like we do with HTML tags. Here is an example of a hyperlink element, nested inside a paragraph element.

```
const url = "https://www.some-store.com";
const buyNow = <p><a href={url}>Buy now</a></p>;
```

To improve code readability, we can write this JSX expression on more than one line. If a JSX expression takes up more than one line, we must wrap the expression in parentheses.

```
const url = "https://www.some-store.com";
const buyNow = (
  <p>
    <a href={url}>Buy now</a>
  </p>
);
```

The JSX outer element rule

JSX has a rule that requires one outermost element for every JSX expression. The following code will result in a JSX error.

```
const text = (
  <p>Paragraph 1.</p>
  <p>Paragraph 2.</p>
);
```

The reason for the error is because the two elements are not wrapped in a containing element. The first opening tag and the final closing tag of a JSX expression must belong to the same JSX element. In this case, the first opening `<p>` tag and the final closing `</p>` tag belong to two different JSX paragraph elements.

We can fix this error by wrapping the two elements in an enclosing tag which will behave as the outermost element.

```
const text = (
  <div className="OutermostElement">
    <p>Paragraph 1.</p>
```

```
  <p>Paragraph 2.</p>
</div>
);
```

The first opening tag and the final closing tag of a JSX expression must belong to the same element.

Whenever a JSX expression has multiple elements, remember to wrap that JSX expression in an outermost element. This outermost element can be any HTML tag, as long as the expression results in valid HTML. For example, a <p> tag in HTML cannot contain another block element within it. That would not be valid HTML.

Fragments

React has a feature called *fragments*. Fragments allow us to wrap a list of child elements within an outer element, but without adding any extra nodes to the DOM.

If we had used fragments in the previous code example above, we would not have had to add the extra `<div>` node to the DOM. We could have saved a DOM node, thus simplifying the DOM tree and making our web application more performant. Here's the previous example re-written using a fragment.

```
import { Fragment } from "react";

const text = (
  <Fragment>
    <p>Paragraph 1.</p>
    <p>Paragraph 2.</p>
  </Fragment>
);
```

There is also a shorter syntax for declaring React fragments. Let's re-write this example using React's short-hand fragment tags.

```
const text = (
  <>
    <p>Paragraph 1.</p>
    <p>Paragraph 2.</p>
  </>
);
```

User-defined components

So far, we've only seen React elements that represent HTML tags. React elements can also represent tags for custom React components that we create.

```
const element = <Greeting />;
```

This React element will render the `Greeting` component to the screen. We can imagine the `Greeting` component to be a React component that displays a greeting to the user.

Recap

This section helped us gain a solid foundation in JSX. We learned what JSX is and how to use it for variables, expressions, HTML attributes, and custom React components. We'll be using everything that we just learned about JSX throughout this book. Let's turn our attention to React components in the next section.

Components

Components are the building blocks of all React apps. Everything in React starts with a component. Think of React components like custom HTML elements.

Components allow us to split up an application's user interface into independent pieces that can be reused throughout a web application. We can work on each component in isolation, without affecting the display of other components.

A component is a small, reusable unit of code. It's job is to return React elements to be displayed on the screen. Each component should be responsible for doing only one thing, and doing it well.

The first letter of a React component must be capitalized. This capitalization differentiates a custom React component from a HTML element like `<h1>`.

There are two ways to write components in React. There are *class components* and there are *functional components*. We'll be focusing on *functional components* because they are more commonly used in modern React development. Functional components are actually just JavaScript functions.

React component lifecycle

A React component can pass through different phases. These phases make up the React component lifecycle. Understanding the lifecycle of a component helps us build more efficient React applications.

Phases of the rendering process

Before understanding the component lifecycle, we must make sure we understand what it means when we say that a component renders, or re-renders. To understand this, let's take a look at the React rendering process. The rendering process is made up of two phases, the rendering phase and the commit phase.

The rendering phase

There are two types of component renders. An initial render and a re-render. This first render happens when a component is displayed on the screen for the first time. A re-render refers to the second render and any other consecutive render of a component that is already displayed on the screen.

> *Component re-renders happen when React needs to update a component with new data. This usually happens as a result of a user interaction, or external data being fetched via an asynchronous request.*

During the rendering phase, React's virtual DOM is created using the React elements returned by the `return` method. The `return` method of a component determines what a component will render. The `return` method returns a component's user interface, expressed in JSX. It is then converted to HTML and added to the virtual DOM tree.

The commit phase

For component re-renders, React compares the new and updated virtual DOM with the previous virtual DOM using a diffing algorithm in order to figure out what changes must be applied to the real DOM. Then, React manipulates the DOM in order to render the user interface to the screen.

For initial renders, there is just one virtual DOM so no diffing algorithm needs to run. The virtual DOM can be applied to the real DOM directly.

Component lifecycle

It's important to know about the React component lifecycle so that we can "hook into" lifecycle events to perform side-effects.

Here are some common side-effects in React that happen during specific lifecycle events.

- We may want to fetch data when a component mounts.
- We may want to change what gets displayed when a component gets updated.
- We may want to notify a parent component when a child component is updated in some way.
- We may need to perform a clean up step just before a component unmounts and is removed from view.

Performing side-effects like these requires us to understand the lifecycle of a component and how to target specific lifecycle events. In later sections, we'll learn how to make use of component lifecycle events to perform side-effects. For now, let's learn all about the React component lifecycle.

The three phases of a component's lifecycle are similar to the circle of life. The first phase is *mounting*, which is like being born. The second phase is *updating*, which is like the changes that occur as we grow into adulthood. The third phase is *unmounting*, which is like dying.

Not every React component goes through all phases. Some components are mounted and never updated. Other components are never unmounted. Let's look at each phase in more detail.

Mounting phase

The mounting phase is when a component is inserted into the DOM. This is where the life of a component begins. It only happens once in a component's life. It is often referred to as the *initial render*.

Updating phase

The updating phase can occur multiple times in a component's life. The updating phase is when a component updates - also known as when a component *re-renders*. A component re-render is triggered in the following cases:

- When the component's internal state is updated.
- When the component's parent re-renders.
- When the value in a Context Provider changes (components that use the context will re-render).
- When the state changes inside a custom Hook (components using it will re-render).

Don't worry about what *context* or *custom Hooks* are right now. We'll get to them later in this book. At this point, remembering the first two points is enough.

Unmounting phase

The unmounting phase is when a component is removed from the DOM.

Our first component

Let's take a look at an example of a very simple React component, called `Greeting`. This component will be defined in a `Greeting.tsx` file. The `Greeting` component's single responsibility is to display a `Hello, world!` greeting.

```
const Greeting = () => <h1>Hello, world!</h1>;

export { Greeting };
```

The `Greeting` component is defined as a JavaScript arrow function that returns a JSX element. Because this arrow function only has one expression, we can omit the curly braces for the function, and write the component on one line.

Here is what the `Greeting` component looks like if we do not omit the curly braces for the arrow function.

```
const Greeting = () => {
  return <h1>Hello, world!</h1>;
};

export { Greeting };
```

We can also use a multi-line return statement by wrapping the element(s) returned in round brackets. Multi-line return statements are useful when our component returns several elements. It's not necessary in this case, but we will see cases where it is needed later.

```
const Greeting = () => {
  return (
    <h1>Hello, world!</h1>
  );
};

export { Greeting };
```

As we've seen from this example, a React component is basically just a JavaScript function that returns React elements. We used an arrow function to create our functional component. We could have also used a traditional JavaScript function to create our functional component. It would give us the the same result.

The `Greeting` component is capitalized, so that when we use it, React will know that it is a custom component that we created, rather than a HTML element. React treats components starting with lowercase letters as HTML elements from the DOM, rather than custom React components. Be sure to always start your React component names with a capital letter.

To use the `Greeting` component in another part of our React application, we first need to import it from the file where it is defined.

```
import { Greeting } from "./Greeting";
```

Once we've imported the Greeting component, we can use it in our JSX code like it's a HTML tag. Let's use the `Greeting` component in another component called `App`.

```
import { Greeting } from './Greeting';

const App = () => {
  return (
    <>
      <Greeting />
      <p>Welcome to my React app!</p>
    </p>
  );
};
```

In this example, the `App` component renders the `Greeting` component and a paragraph element within a React fragment. The App component renders a large "Hello, world!" heading, followed by a paragraph with the text, "Welcome to my React app!".

Since the App component uses the `Greeting` component, it is considered the *parent* component for `Greeting`, and `Greeting` is considered a *child* of the App component.

We can use the `Greeting` component with an opening and closing tag, `<Greeting></Greeting>`. Or, we can use it with a self-closing tag, `<Greeting />` for short. Always use self-closing tags for React components, unless there are elements that need to be passed within the opening and closing tags. We'll learn more about this special case later.

In it's current state, the `Greeting` component is not very flexible. No matter where we use this component, it will always display the same message. We can make this component customizable with the help of *props*.

Props

Components can accept inputs, called *props* (short for "properties"). When one component needs to pass information to another component, it will use that component's props.

> *An example of information sharing between components is when a parent component needs to pass information to a child component. We call a component a child component when it is part of another component and rendered by that component. The component that renders it is referred to as its parent.*

A component's props is an object that contains data used by the component. When it comes to their props, React components behave like *pure* functions. This means that React components must never modify their own props. Props are read-only.

Component props are similar to attributes on HTML tags, such as the `type` attribute on the HTML `input` tag.

```
<input type="text" />
```

Component props allow us to configure and customize our React components.

Using props

Let's re-write the `Greeting` component using props. This will allow us to customize the greeting message that the component displays.

```
type Props = {
  name: string;
};

const Greeting = (props: Props) => {
  return <p>Hello, {props.name}!</p>;
};

export { Greeting };
```

A component's *props* is just a JavaScript object. Using TypeScript, we can give the props a type. In this example, we specified that our props object will have a required `name` property of type `string`. Any component that wants to use the `Greeting` prop, will be required to pass it a `name`.

We now have a `Greeting` component that won't just display a static message every time it is used. Instead, it can be customized to greet any person by name.

Let's make use of this customizable `Greeting` component in the `App` component.

```
import { Greeting } from "./Greeting";

const App = () => {
  const name = "John Smith";

  return <Greeting name={name} />;
};

export { App };
```

The App component will render "Hello, John Smith!" to the screen.

When passing variables, arrays, or objects as props, we wrap them in curly braces, as we did with `name={name}`. We could have also passed the person's name directly to the name prop, by doing `name='John Smith'`.

Rather than giving the App component the responsibility of displaying a greeting, we have taken this responsibility and extracted it to its own component, called `Greeting`.

A single React app can contain hundreds of components. Each component might be small and unimpressive on its own. However, when combined, these components can make up a great looking, feature-rich, user interface.

Using props with destructuring

We can re-write the `Greeting` component to make use of the JavaScript object destructuring syntax. This will allow us to pick out the exact object properties that we want to use in our component.

```
type Props = {
  name: string;
};

const Greeting = ({ name }: Props) => {
  return <h1>Hello, {name}!</h1>;
};

export { Greeting };
```

Destructuring makes using component props less verbose. We no longer have to refer to the name property as `props.name`. We can simply refer to it as `name`.

TypeScript props

Using TypeScript, React props can be represented using either *type aliases* or *interfaces*. Both are very similar. In most cases, you can go with either one.

Almost all features of an interface are also available with a type alias. The main difference is that new fields can always be added to an already existing interface, but the same is not true for type aliases. However, re-opening an interface to add new properties to it is not commonly done. Therefore, we will stick to using type aliases for this book.

```
// type alias
type Props = {
  name: string;
};

// interface
interface Props {
  name: string;
}
```

Child-to-parent communication

We just learned how props allow parent-to-child communication between React components. Now, let's see how child components can pass data to their parent components.

We can also use props to pass functions to a component. This allows a parent component to pass a *callback function* down to a child component. The child component can then notify the parent of any internal changes within it by calling the parent component's function that it received in its props.

In JavaScript, a callback function is a function passed into another function as an argument. The function passed in can then be invoked by the function that receives it. React components are just JavaScript function, therefore, a function passed into a component is known as a callback function.

Let's take a look at two examples of child-to-parent communication. The first example will not pass any parameters, while the second example will.

Without passing parameters

In this example, we'll define a parent component, called `Tweets`, that will reference a child component called `Tweet`. We would like the parent component to be notified when a user clicks the "favorite" button in the child component.

Let's add an `onFavorite` prop to the `Tweet` component. We will prefix it with on to identify it as a prop that expects to receive a callback function. Using TypeScript, we will type the `onFavorite` prop to be a function that returns nothing (`void`).

```
type Props = {
  onFavorite: () => void;
};

const Tweet = ({ onFavorite }: Props) => {
  return (
    <div>
      <p>This is a Tweet</p>
      <button onClick={onFavorite}>Favorite</button>
    </div>
  );
};
```

```
const Tweets = () => {
  const handleOnFavorite = () => {
    alert("Parent received a favorite event.");
  };

  return <Tweet onFavorite={handleOnFavorite} />;
};

export { Tweets };
```

When we make use of the Tweet component in the Tweets component, we give the Tweet component's onFavorite prop the name of a callback function defined in the parent component, handleOnFavorite. The handleOnFavorite callback function will be triggered whenever the "Favorite" button in the Tweet component is clicked.

Every time the "Favorite" button is clicked, an alert will be displayed with the message, "Parent received a favorite event." The alert is produced by the parent component for an event that happened in a child component.

For the sake of readability, we kept both the Tweet and Tweets components in the same file, but we could have also placed them in their own respective files.

Passing no function parameters via the onFavorite prop is fine when there is only one Tweet component used in the Tweets component. However, what if there were multiple Tweet components used? How would our parent component know which specific Tweet was favorited? We can solve this by passing function parameters via the onFavorite prop.

With parameters passed

Let's take a look at how to pass parameters when communicating from a child component to a parent component. Let's say that we want our parent component, Tweets, to know the id of the tweet that was favorited by a user. What would the code for that look like? Let's take a look.

```
type Props = {
  id: number;
  text: string;
  onFavorite: (id: number) => void;
};

const Tweet = ({ id, text, onFavorite }: Props) => {
  return (
```

```
    <div>
      <p>{text}</p>
      <button onClick={() => onFavorite(id)}>Favorite</button>
    </div>
  );
};

const Tweets = () => {
  const handleOnFavorite = (id: number) => {
    alert(`Favorite event for Tweet ${id}`);
  };

  return (
    <>
      <Tweet id={1} text={"Tweet 1"} onFavorite={handleOnFavorite} />
      <Tweet id={2} text={"Tweet 2"} onFavorite={handleOnFavorite} />
    </>
  );
};

export { Tweets };
```

Notice that we updated the type for the onFavorite prop on the Tweet component to include a function parameter id of type number. Passing an id parameter from the child component to the parent component will allow us to know exactly which child component was just favorited.

The onClick event on the button of the Tweet component was updated from onClick={onFavorite} to onClick={() => onFavorite(id)}. We used an inline arrow function in the onClick event so that we can pass the id parameter to the callback function. Whenever we need to pass a parameter to a callback function that is received as a prop, we use an inline arrow function.

The parent component's handleOnFavorite function was updated to receive the id of the tweet that was favorited.

When we click on the "Favorite" button for "Tweet 1", it produces an alert that says, "Favorite event for Tweet 1". When we click on the "Favorite" button for "Tweet 2", it produces an alert that says, "Favorite event for Tweet 2".

Events

React makes it easy to handle events that take place in the DOM, such as click events, mouseover events, key press events, form events, and more.

Handling events with React elements is similar to handling events on DOM elements. However, the syntax is a bit different.

React events are named using camelCase, rather than the lowercase naming that is used with HTML. With JSX, a function is passed as the event handler, rather than the string that is used with HTML.

The HTML for handling an `onclick` event on a `button` element in the DOM looks like the following.

```
<button onclick="handleClick()">Click me</button>
```

Handling the same event is slightly different in React. `onclick` becomes `onClick`, and `handleClick()` becomes `handleClick`.

```
<button onClick={handleClick}>Click me</button>
```

Inline event handler function

Let's take a look at an example of a `Button` component that uses the `onClick` event.

```
const Button = () => {
  return <button onClick={() => console.log("Clicked")}>Submit</button>;
};

export { Button };
```

Event handler functions are what we assign to the value of an event like `onClick`. In this example, an inline arrow function is used as the event handler function.

When the button element is clicked, the event handler function passed to the `onClick` event, is fired. Clicking on the "Submit" button prints "Clicked" to the console.

Event handler function outside of JSX

We can also declare event handler functions outside of JSX.

```
import { MouseEvent } from "react";
```

```
const Button = () => {
  const handleClickEvent = (event: MouseEvent<HTMLButtonElement>) => {
    console.log(`Event type: ${event.type}`);
  };

  return <button onClick={handleClickEvent}>Submit</button>;
};

export { Button };
```

In this example, the `handleClickEvent` event handler function is defined outside of the JSX that is returned by the `Button` component. For more complex event handler functions that are more than one line long, this is the ideal approach.

Using TypeScript, we defined a type for the `event` argument of the event handler function. We specified that this function will receive events of type `MouseEvent` from a `HTMLButtonElement`.

When we use an inline event handler, we don't need to add a type for the event like we did here. TypeScript will infer the event type in such cases.

onClick is not just for buttons

The `onClick` event can be added to any React element - not just buttons. Let's take a look at an example that adds the `onClick` event to a `<div>` tag rather than a `<button>`.

```
import { MouseEvent } from "react";

const Button = () => {
  const handleClickEvent = (event: MouseEvent<HTMLDivElement>) => {
    console.log(`Event type: ${event.type}`);
  };

  return <div onClick={handleClickEvent}>Submit</div>;
};

export { Button };
```

In the same `Button` component that we saw earlier, the `<button>` was swapped out for a `<div>`. The type of event received by the event handler function was updated to a `MouseEvent` of type `HTMLDivElement`. This is because the event handler function now receives a mouse event from a `<div>` element rather than a `<button>` element.

Async event handlers for onClick

Event handlers, or event handler functions, don't always have to be synchronous. We can create asynchronous event handlers for events like `onClick`. This allows us to make an asynchronous request to fetch data when a user click event occurs.

Let's take a look at an example of an asynchronous event handler. We'll start by by creating a React component where we will define a button with an `onClick` event. Then we'll add an `async` event handler for it. Clicking on the button will fetch and display a list of todo items.

```
const API_URL = 'https://jsonplaceholder.typicode.com/todos';

type Todo = {
  id: number;
  title: string;
  completed: boolean;
};

const Todos = () => {
  const [todos, setTodos] = useState<Todo[]>([]);

  const handleClick = async () => {
    try {
      const response = await fetch(API_URL);

      const data = await response.json();

      setTodos(data);
    } catch (error) {
      console.log(`Error: ${error}`);
    }
  };

  return (
    <div>
      <button onClick={handleClick}>Show Todos</button>
      {todos.length > 0 && (
        <ul>
          {todos.map(({ id, title }) => (
            <li key={id}>{title}</li>
          ))}
        </ul>
      )}
    </div>
  );
};
```

```
export { Todos };
```

The `handleClick` function is an `async` (asynchronous) function that uses the *Fetch API* to request data from an API endpoint. The API endpoint that we used returns a list of todo items that we store in the component's state with the `setTodos` state setter function. After the data fetching is complete, a list of `todos` is rendered to the screen.

Don't worry if you're not yet familiar with component state. It will be covered in an upcoming chapter. The example above was just to show that event handler functions can also be asynchronous.

React support for events

React supports many types of events, such as, `onBlur`, `onFocus`, `onKeyDown`, `onKeyUp`, `onChange`, `onSubmit`, etc. We'll get the chance to see more examples with events later on in this book. For now, let's simply go over descriptions for the events listed.

- onBlur: Triggered when an element loses focus, such as when a user clicks outside of a form input after having clicked inside it. This event is sometimes used to validate a form input, providing immediate feedback to the user. The TypeScript type for this event is `FocusEvent<HTML...Element>`, where `...` corresponds to the type of element emitting the event (ex: `HTMLInputElement`).

- onFocus: Triggered when an element receives focus, such as when a user clicks inside a form input. The TypeScript type for this event is `FocusEvent<HTML...Element>`, where `...` corresponds to the type of element emitting the event (ex: `HTMLInputElement`).

- onKeyDown: Triggered when a keyboard key is pressed down. The TypeScript type for this event is `KeyboardEvent<HTML...Element>`, where `...` corresponds to the type of element emitting the event (ex: `HTMLInputElement`).

- onKeyUp: Triggered when a keyboard key is released after being pressed down. The TypeScript type for this event is `KeyboardEvent<HTML...Element>`, where `...` corresponds to the type of element emitting the event (ex: `HTMLInputElement`).

- onChange: Triggered when the value of an input element changes. It is typically used to detect changes in form input elements. The TypeScript type for this event is

ChangeEvent<HTML...Element>, where ... corresponds to the type of element emitting the event (ex: HTMLInputElement).

- onSubmit: Triggered when the user submits a form, either by clicking a submit button or by pressing the *Enter* key while focused on a form field. The TypeScript type for this event is FormEvent<HTMLFormElement>.

The children prop

React has a special prop called children. The children prop will contain the value of anything that is passed between the opening and closing tags of a component.

Suppose we have a Sidebar component with a children prop. The children prop allows us to do something like this.

```
<Sidebar>Hello World</Sidebar>
```

This will cause the Sidebar component to render "Hello World" wherever its children prop is rendered in the JSX that it returns.

Let's take a look at the Sidebar component to see how the children prop works.

```
import { ReactNode } from "react";

type Props = {
  children?: ReactNode;
};

const Sidebar = ({ children }: Props) => {
  return <div>{children}</div>;
};

export { Sidebar };
```

TypeScript allows us to specify a type for the children prop in the Sidebar component. We used the type ReactNode because it has a wide range of support for many types of elements.

We used a ? when defining the type for children in order to make it an optional prop for the Sidebar component. This way, if no children are passed to the Sidebar component, no error will be thrown. It will simply render empty <div></div> tags.

When to use the children prop

The children prop comes in handy for components that don't know exactly what they will receive ahead of time. This usually happens for more generic components, such as Layout, Sidebar, or Dialog. These components behave like generic boxes for content. Generic components like these can use the special children prop to render any child elements that are passed to them. Using this strategy is referred to as *containment* in React.

The React children prop helps us to easily create reusable components because it allows components to be constructed together. We can put any amount of components within the children "slot". It's that flexible!

Let's take a look at a more realistic example of a Sidebar component that makes use of the special children prop.

```
import { ReactNode } from "react";

type Props = {
  title: string;
  children?: ReactNode;
};

const Sidebar = ({ title, children }: Props) => {
  return (
    <div>
      <h3>{title}</h3>
      {children}
    </div>
  );
};

const SidebarMenu = () => {
  return (
    <ul>
      <li>Item 1</li>
    </ul>
  );
};

const App = () => {
  return (
    <>
      <Sidebar title="Sidebar">
        <SidebarMenu />
        <div>
```

```
            <h3>A widget</h3>
            <p>This is a widget.</p>
          </div>
          <p>Thanks for using the sidebar.</p>
        </Sidebar>
      </>
    );
};

export { App };
```

The App component passes three children to the `Sidebar` component. The first child is a React component that we created, called `SidebarMenu`. The other two children are defined using the `<div>` and `<p>` HTML tags, respectively. This is to show that the `children` prop is flexible enough to receive React components that we create, as well as elements defined with HTML tags.

This is the same `Sidebar` component from the previous example, but with an extra prop called `title`. This was done in order to show that the `children` prop can exist alongside many other props. The only difference between the `children` prop and other props is the way that we pass data to the `children` prop. The data that we want to pass to the `children` prop gets embedded between the component's opening and closing tags.

Multiple children

Sometimes, we might need to define multiple slots for a component. Rather than using the `children` prop, we can define our own props for this.

Here is an example of a `Panel` component with two slots, `left` and `right`. Both slots are defined using the `ReactNode` type.

```
import { ReactNode } from "react";

type Props = {
  left: ReactNode;
  right: ReactNode;
};

const Panel = ({ left, right }: Props) => {
  return (
    <div>
      <div>{left}</div>
      <div>{right}</div>
    </div>
```

```
  );
};

const Profile = () => {
  return <p>Profile</p>;
};

const ContactForm = () => {
  return <p>Contact form</p>;
};

const App = () => {
  return <Panel left={<Profile />} right={<ContactForm />} />;
};

export { App };
```

Using multiple slots, rather than one children slot, allows us to be more flexible with the layout and positioning of elements.

<Profile /> and <ContactForm /> are React elements, and we learned earlier that they're really just JavaScript objects. This means that we can pass them as props, just as we do with simpler data types, such as strings and numbers. There's no limit to what we can pass as props in React.

Conditional rendering

React components that we build will often need to display different elements depending on different conditions. This means that we can choose to render different components, styles, or data depending on whether a condition is met or not.

In React, we can conditionally render elements using a few different approaches. Let's take a look at them.

Conditionally rendering nothing

In some cases, we might want some React components to hide themselves and not render, even if they were rendered by another component. To do so, we can simply return `null` from the component.

Let's consider a React component called `OrderItem` that receives info about an order item and renders it on the screen. If an item is not shipped yet, we don't want the `OrderItem` component to render anything. A React component must always return something, so we'll still need a return statement within `OrderItem`. When the `isShipped` prop on the `OrderItem` component is `false`, we will return `null`. Returning `null` will cause the `OrderItem` component not to render.

```
type Props = {
  name: string;
  isShipped?: boolean;
};

const OrderItem = ({ name, isShipped }: Props) => {
  if (!isShipped) {
    return null;
  }

  return <p>{name}</p>;
};

export { OrderItem };
```

The `isShipped` prop is defined as an optional prop. This means that `isShipped` can either be `false` or `undefined`. Both are *falsy* cases and will be caught by the `if` statement in the `OrderItem` component.

Returning null from a component isn't the greatest solution. Since the component can *sometimes* render nothing, it can be a confusing component to reuse and debug.

The better solution is to conditionally include or exclude a component directly from the parent component. Suppose the parent component of OrderItem is Order, then the Order component would be the one to conditionally include OrderItem if isShipped is true. With this solution, we would no longer have to return null from OrderItem.

Conditionally rendering with if statements

We can conditionally return different JSX expressions from components based on whether a condition is met or not. To do so, we can use traditional JavaScript if statements outside of JSX expressions in order to handle different conditions.

```
type Props = {
  name: string;
  isShipped?: boolean;
};

const OrderItem = ({ name, isShipped }: Props) => {
  if (isShipped) {
    return <p>{name} (shipped)</p>;
  }

  return <p>{name}</p>;
};

const Order = () => {
  return (
    <section>
      <OrderItem name="iPhone" isShipped={false} />
      <OrderItem name="iPad" isShipped={true} />
      <OrderItem name="iMac" isShipped />
    </section>
  );
};

export { Order };
```

The OrderItem component for the "iPhone" has its isShipped prop set to false. The other OrderItem components both have their isShipped prop set to true.

When we want to set a prop to be true, we can do it explicitly as, isShipped={true}, or we can do it implicitly, by just including the isShipped prop.

68

When the `isShipped` prop is `true`, the `OrderItem` component returns a JSX expression that includes a status of "shipped" beside the name of the item ordered.

The only issue with the approach used in this example is that we have code duplication in the `OrderItem` component. There are two `return` statements that both return paragraph elements. Can we do better? Yes we can. Let's see how.

Rather than returning directly from the `if` statement, as we did in the `OrderItem` component above, we can use a variable. The variable will be assigned the right elements to return, and then the component will return the variable. This will help us reduce the amount of code duplication.

In JavaScript, defining variables with `let` allows us to reassign variables defined with it. Let's define a variable with `let` and assign it the default text that we want to render, which is the name of the order item.

```
type Props = {
  name: string;
  isShipped?: boolean;
};

const OrderItem = ({ name, isShipped }: Props) => {
  let result = name;

  if (isShipped) {
    result = `${name} (shipped)`;
  }

  return <p>{result}</p>;
};

export { OrderItem };
```

If we enter the `if` statement in `OrderItem`, we reassign a JSX expression to the `result` variable that we defined, indicated that the item has shipped. The `OrderItem` component now only has one `return` statement that returns whatever has been assigned to the `result` variable.

This approach to conditional rendering involves a few more lines of code, but it provides more flexibility and reduces the amount of code duplication.

Conditional rendering within JSX

We can also conditionally render things using JavaScript directly within JSX expressions. We'll look at two different ways of doing this. The first approach will use the *ternary* operator. The second approach will use the logical AND operator.

The ternary operator

Let's use the ternary operator within the JSX of the element returned by the `OrderItem` component. We will use it to check if an order item has been shipped.

```
type Props = {
  name: string;
  isShipped?: boolean;
};

const OrderItem = ({ name, isShipped }: Props) => {
  return <p>{isShipped ? `${name} (shipped)` : name}</p>;
};

export { OrderItem };
```

This approach is fine for simple conditions, but we should avoid using it for more complex conditions. We should also not use it too often in the same component. It can bloat our components with too much conditional markup that can be hard to trace and debug.

If we find ourselves using too many ternary operators within one component, we should consider splitting that component up into separate components. This can help us better organize the conditional logic.

We can also include HTML tags or React component tags within ternary expressions. Let's say we want the order item's name to appear in bold if it has shipped. Here's how we would do that within the ternary expression.

```
type Props = {
  name: string;
  isShipped?: boolean;
};

const OrderItem = ({ name, isShipped }: Props) => {
  return <p>{isShipped ? <strong>{`${name} (shipped)`}</strong> : name}</p>;
};
```

```
export { OrderItem };
```

The logical AND operator (&&)

The logical AND operator allows us to render an element within a JSX expression based on a boolean condition. The logical AND operator is great for conditional expressions that will sometimes do something, but other times do nothing at all - because a certain condition has not been met.

If the expression on the left of the && evaluates to `true`, then the JSX expression on the right of the && will be rendered. If the expression on the left of the && is `false`, then the JSX expression to the right of the && will not be rendered. React treats `false` as a gap in the JSX tree, just like `null` or `undefined`, and will not render anything in its place.

Let's use the logical AND operator to create a conditional expression for the shipping status of an order item in the `OrderItem` component.

```
type Props = {
  name: string;
  isShipped?: boolean;
};

const OrderItem = ({ name, isShipped }: Props) => {
  return (
    <p>
      {name} {isShipped && " (shipped)"}
    </p>
  );
};

export { OrderItem };
```

We can read the && operator like a *then* for the `if` condition. If `isShipped` is `true`, then (&&) render the "shipped" label beside the order item name. Otherwise, don't render the "shipped" label.

This example was a good case for the logical AND operator because the conditional check only needs to display something when `isShipped` is `true`. We do not need anything to be displayed when `isShipped` is `false`. The conditional logic is simple enough to be handled with the logical AND operator.

When using the logical AND operator, there's no `else` case. If we do want to handle an `else` case with the logical AND operator when `isShipped` is `false`, we could do the following.

```
type Props = {
  name: string;
  isShipped?: boolean;
};

const OrderItem = ({ name, isShipped }: Props) => {
  return (
    <p>
      {name} {isShipped && " (shipped)"} {!isShipped && " (not shipped)"}
    </p>
  );
};

export { OrderItem };
```

As you can see, this introduces redundancy within the OrderItem component. The else case is better handled using the *if statement* or the *ternary operator* approaches that we saw earlier.

The ternary operator allows us to rewrite the if and else cases that we used above in a single one-line expression.

```
type Props = {
  name: string;
  isShipped?: boolean;
};

const OrderItem = ({ name, isShipped }: Props) => {
  return <p>{isShipped ? `${name} (shipped)` : `${name} (not shipped)`}</p>;
};

export { OrderItem };
```

The logical AND operator pitfall

Avoid putting numbers on the left side of the logical AND operator. JavaScript will automatically convert the left side of a logical AND expression to a boolean. However, if the left side of that expression is zero, then the whole expression gets the value zero. React will end up rendering zero rather than nothing. Many React developers make this common mistake. Let's take a look at an example.

```
type Props = {
  ordersCount: number;
};

const OrdersPage = ({ ordersCount }: Props) => {
  return <div>{ordersCount && <h4>Orders</h4>}</div>;
};
```

```
export { OrdersPage };
```

The common assumption is that nothing will get rendered when `ordersCount` is 0. However, what actually gets rendered by the `OrdersPage` component is the value 0.

To fix this mistake, we must make the left side of the logical AND expression a boolean expression. We can do this by using JavaScript's *greater than* comparison operator.

```
type Props = {
  ordersCount: number;
};

const OrdersPage = ({ ordersCount }: Props) => {
  return <div>{ordersCount > 0 && <h4>Orders</h4>}</div>;
};

export { OrdersPage };
```

Now, nothing will be rendered by the `OrdersPage` component if the value passed to the `ordersCount` prop is 0 or less. We'll no longer see a surprise 0 value.

Iterating and looping

Iterating (or looping) to displaying data is a common part of every application. Iterating (or looping) allows us to programmatically render a list of items, without having to hard-code each one.

The hard-coded approach

```
const MainMenu = () => {
  return (
    <ul>
      <li>Home</li>
      <li>About</li>
      <li>Contact</li>
    </ul>
  );
};

export { MainMenu };
```

We can easily hard-code a list of items. However, what if the list of items were in an array that gets passed into the component via props? We won't be able to hard-code that sort of list in the component. How then will we iterate over an array like `['Home', 'About', 'Contact']` and create `<li>` elements for each item in the array?

One great thing about React is that it doesn't require us to learn new ways to iterate and loop over data. Instead, React allows us to use JavaScript for this common task. We can use JavaScript's map method to easily iterate over an array and create a new one with the values we need.

Using JavaScript's map() method

When we need to create a list of JSX elements from a JavaScript array, the JavaScript map method is very helpful. The map method will allow us to iterate over each item in the array and return a JSX element for each one.

```
const MainMenu = () => {
  const items = ['Home', 'About', 'Contact'];

  return (
    <ul>
      {items.map(item => <li>{item}</li>)}
    </ul>
  );
};
```

```
export { MainMenu };
```

We can also assign the result of the map function to a variable and then use that variable within the return statement.

```
const MainMenu = () => {
  const items = ['Home', 'About', 'Contact'];
  const menuItems = items.map(item => <li>{item}</li>);

  return (
    <ul>{menuItems}</ul>
  );
};

export { MainMenu };
```

This approach simplifies the return statement for the MainMenu component. It's especially helpful in cases where the map operation is more complex than just a one-line expression.

Now that our MainMenu supports programmatic iteration rather than hard-coded display, let's update MainMenu to receive an array of strings as props.

```
type Props = {
  items: string[];
};

const MainMenu = ({ items }: Props) => {
  const menuItems = items.map(item => <li>{item}</li>);

  return (
    <ul>{menuItems}</ul>
  );
};

export { MainMenu };
```

We can now use the MainMenu component by passing an array of items to it via its items prop.

```
const App = () => {
  return (
    <MainMenu items={['Home', 'About', 'Contact']} />
  );
};

export { App };
```

Returning from map()

In cases where the elements returned by the JavaScript map method span multiple lines, we can either use an implicit return or an explicit return.

Implicit return

An implicit return can be used when there is no extra logic that needs to be done within the map method.

```
type MenuItem = {
  name: string;
  description: string;
};

type Props = {
  items: MenuItem[];
};

const MainMenu = ({ items }: Props) => {
  const menuItems = items.map(({ name, description }) => (
    <li>
      <h4>{name}</h4>
      <p>{description}</p>
    </li>
  ));

  return (
    <ul>{menuItems}</ul>
  );
};

export { MainMenu };
```

In this example, we made the items prop receive an array of MenuItem objects with a name and description. Each menu item will have a name and a description. This was done in order to show how to iterate with map on multiple lines and use an implicit return. The implicit return uses round brackets, (...) around the multi-line elements that map will return.

We used destructuring within map to make the individual object properties of name and description directly available to us in each iteration. If we did not use destructuring, we would have needed to reference the object properties as item.name and item.description.

Explicit return

An explicit return can be used when the code within the map method does more than just return elements. Perhaps there is some embedded logic within the map, followed by the actual return statement.

Here is an example of an explicit return within the map method.

```
type MenuItem = {
  name: string;
  description: string;
};

type Props = {
  items: MenuItem[];
};

const MainMenu = ({ items }: Props) => {
  const menuItems = items.map(({ name, description }) => {
    const nameUppercase = name.toUpperCase();

    return (
      <li>
        <h4>{nameUppercase}</h4>
        <p>{description}</p>
      </li>
    );
  });

  return (
    <ul>{menuItems}</ul>
  );
};

export { MainMenu };
```

In this example, additional logic is performed with each iteration of the items array to make the name uppercase before returning the name and description for each menu item. As a result, we used curly brackets within map to accommodate the additional logic. We then included an explicit return statement within the curly brackets.

Remember that the JavaScript map method will always return an array. We just get to choose how to write out the return syntax within map - either implicitly or explicitly, depending on the scenario.

77

Keys

The `MainMenu` component examples above will cause the following React error to be displayed in the browser's developer console.

```
Warning: Each child in a list should have a unique "key" prop.
```

React requires that a key attribute be added to uniquely identify each element in a list. This will help React to identify which items changed, were added, or removed from the list. They key is declared within a tag just like any other attribute is.

Keys help with performance because they allow React to keep track of which list items need to be re-rendered due to changes. They are also important for keeping track of the order of items in the list.

Let's re-write the `MainMenu` component using keys in order to fix the warning message.

```
type Props = {
  items: string[];
};

const MainMenu = ({ items }: Props) => {
  const menuItems = items.map(item => <li key={item}>{item}</li>);

  return (
    <ul>{menuItems}</ul>
  );
};

export { MainMenu };
```

Avoid index as a key

It's common to see code where the `index` of the `map` method is used for list item keys.

```
const menuItems = items.map((item, index) =>
  <li key={index}>
    {item}
  </li>
);
```

React does not recommend using indexes for keys, especially if the order of items may change. Using indexes can lead to unexpected behavior and performance issues.

Keys should be given only to the JSX elements generated by the map method on the array. The best way to pick a key is to use a unique identifier for each item among its siblings. It does not need to be a globally unique identifier. It only needs to be unique among an item's siblings. The unique identifier could be an ID from a database, a unique property of an item, or a unique combination of item properties.

If an array does not have a stable id per item provided by a database, we can use the crypto.randomUUID method. The crypto.randomUUID method is provided by major web browsers to generate unique keys for items. This method will create a randomly generated, 36 character long unique string. Using this method, we can guarantee that each item in the list gets a unique ID.

We must be careful not to use crypto.randomUUID to generate IDs on the fly.

```
// Do not do this!
<ul>
  {items.map(item => {
    return (
      <li key={crypto.randomUUID()}>{item}</li>
    );
  })}
</ul>
```

Generating the ID directly in iterations of map will make the key change on every component render. Every time the key changes, the corresponding element will be recreated by React. This slows down performance and causes any user input associated to a list item with a specific key to be lost.

We should create a new array of objects with an id property populated by crypto.randomUUID. After unique IDs have been associated to each array item, we can then render the new array. Let's see what that looks like.

```
type Props = {
  items: string[];
}

const Menu = ({ items }: Props) => {
  const itemsWithIds = items.map(item => {
    return {
      id: crypto.randomUUID(),
      name: item,
    };
  });
```

```
    return (
      <ul>
        {itemsWithIds.map(({ id, name }) => {
          return (
            <li key={id}>{name}</li>
          );
        })}
      </ul>
    );
}

export { Menu };
```

Keys are not props

Keys are not props. Keys are an internal hint to React but they don't actually get passed into components as props. If we need the value of a key in a component, we will need to pass it explicitly as a prop with a different name.

```
type MenuItem = {
  id: number;
  name: string;
  description: string;
};

type Props = {
  items: MenuItem[];
};

const Item = ({ id, name, description }: MenuItem) => {
  return (
    <li>
      <h5>{id}: {name}</h5>
      <p>{description}</p>
    </li>
  );
}

const MainMenu = ({ items }: Props) => {
  const menuItems = items.map(({ id, name, description }) => (
    <Item
      key={id}
      id={id}
      name={name}
      description={description} />
  ));

  return (
```

```
      <ul>{menuItems}</ul>
  );
};

export { MainMenu };
```

The Item component will have no access to key. This is because key is not a prop. Therefore, we defined an id prop that will receive the same value that we used for key. We cannot rely on key to get the id value within the Item component, so we defined the id prop to handle that for us.

Rather than explicitly writing out a closing tag, this example used the shorthand syntax when using Item. It's quicker to write <Item /> rather than <Item></Item>, and it results in less code.

Fragments and keys

React fragments using the Fragment tags can have keys. Here is an example of a situation where fragments with keys may be useful.

```
import { Fragment } from "react";

type Term = {
  id: number;
  name: string;
  description: string;
};

type Props = {
  terms: Array<Term>;
};

const Glossary = ({ terms }: Props) => {
  return (
    <dl>
      {terms.map((term) => (
        <Fragment key={term.id}>
          <dt>{term.name}</dt>
          <dd>{term.description}</dd>
        </Fragment>
      ))}
    </dl>
  );
};

export { Glossary };
```

In this example, we built a description list `<dl></dl>` with terms `<dt></dt>` and descriptions `<dd></dd>`. We received an array of `terms` as a prop for our `Glossary` component and mapped it to an array of fragments that get displayed as a description list.

Description lists `<dl>` don't tend to use elements other than `<dt>` and `<dd>`. However, we still needed an element to wrap them both. This is because of the JSX rule that requires one outermost containing element. This made React fragments very helpful here.

Let's make use of the `Glossary` component by passing it an array of glossary terms and their descriptions.

```
const App = () => {
  return (
    <Glossary terms={[
        { id: 1, name: 'React', description: 'A JavaScript library' },
        { id: 2, name: 'Vite', description: 'Frontend tooling' },
        { id: 3, name: 'JavaScript', description: 'A scripting language' },
      ]}
    />
  );
};

export { App };
```

Recap

This section laid a very important foundation of knowledge that rest of the book will build upon. We learned all about the building blocks of React applications, components!

- An initial render happens when a component is displayed on the screen for the first time.
- A re-render happens when a component that is already displayed on the screen, is updated.
- A component's lifecycle consists of a mounting phase, an updating phase, and an unmounting phase.
- Props allow us to pass data to components and communicate between components.
- The special `children` prop is handy for building generic components. We can also configure multiple slots for a component.
- We can conditionally render content within a JSX expression using the ternary operator or the logical AND operator.
- We can use JavaScript `if` statements, outside of JSX, to conditionally render content from a component.
- JavaScript's `map` method is a convenient way to iterate over arrays in React components.
- A key attribute is required on every element generated by iterating over arrays. Keys are not like regular props.
- The `index` provided by the `map` method is not a good choice for a key.

Fundamental Hooks

React Hooks were added to React in version 16.8 and intended for use within functional components. Prior to version 16.8 of React, class components were used to access lifecycle events, and it was more complicated to do so. Hooks simplified the usage of lifecycle events within components.

Hooks are just JavaScript functions that allow us to "hook into" React features, such as state and lifecycle events.

Hooks are functions that must start with the keyword "use". Hooks can only be called at the top level of a component, or within our own custom Hooks. If we want to *use* a hook, we must use it at the top of our component. It's similar to how we can only import modules at the top of a file.

Though they are functions, Hooks can't be called inside conditional expressions, loops, or nested functions. This ensures that Hooks are always called in the same order every time a component renders. Order is important for Hooks. If we conditionally render Hooks, the order in which they are called cannot be guaranteed between component renders.

This book has three sections dedicated to React Hooks. This section covers the fundamental Hooks that are most commonly used. The next section covers performance-related Hooks, and the last section covers custom Hooks. React also has a context Hook that we'll learn about in a later section dedicated to context.

The fundamental React Hooks that will be covered in this section are the following.

- **State Hooks:** `useState` and `useReducer` allow React components to "remember" information.
- **Ref Hooks:** `useRef` allows React components to "remember" information independent of state.
- **Effect Hooks:** `useEffect` allows React components to connect to external systems such as the network and the browser DOM.

The useState Hook

Components often need to change what they display to the screen when they are interacted with. Here are some examples of user interactions that make changes to the user interface.

- Clicking a "Next" button must navigate to the next page.
- A text input field must be updated to display the input that the user is typing into it.
- Clicking on a collapsible menu needs to open and close it.

For components to change what they display after they are interacted with, components need to have a good memory. They need to remember things.

A page component needs to remember what page of results we're on and how many total pages there are. A text input component needs to remember the current value that the user entered. A menu component needs to remember if was opened or if it's still closed. In React, this internal component-specific memory is called *state*. We can think of state as data that changes over time.

Can we just use a local variable?

At this point, you might be wondering why we can't just use a local variable instead of this thing called *state*. That's a great question.

The issue with local variables is that they won't be persisted when a component re-renders. When React renders a component for a second time, after some change occurred, it won't remember the value that was assigned to a local variable before the second render occurred. Also, when we make a change to a local variable, it won't trigger a re-render of the component. React doesn't interpret a change to a local variable as a reason to render the component again. It's not a signal to React that there is new data to be displayed by the component.

To make changes to a component's data and to display that new data, we must preserve data between component re-renders, and then we must tell React to re-render the component. Thankfully, we don't have to do all this manually. The React `useState` Hook gives us exactly what we need. It provides us with a state variable to preserve data between re-renders, and a state setter function to update the state variable. The `useState` Hook also informs React to re-render the component after a state variable has been updated, so that the new state variable's value can be displayed.

Using the useState Hook

Let's define a `Counter` component. Within it, let's use the `useState` Hook to keep track of a count value that we want to allow users to increment.

```
import { useState } from 'react';

const Counter = () => {
  const [count, setCount] = useState<number>(0);

  const increment = () => setCount(count + 1);

  return <button onClick={increment}>{count}</button>;
};

export { Counter };
```

When we use the `useState` hook, it's because we want our component to have a good memory and remember something. In this example, we want our `Counter` component to remember the value of `count`.

The argument passed to the `useState` hook is the initial value of the state variable `count`. The initial value of `count` is set to 0. TypeScript allows us to specify the type of the state variable. The type of the `count` state variable was defined to be a `number`.

Every time the `Counter` component renders, the `useState` hook will provide us with an array containing two values, the state variable (`count`), and the state setter function (`setCount`). We will use the state setter function to update `count` and re-render our component.

The `useState` Hook always returns a pair. The naming within the array can be anything we want. However, if we name the second variable in the array using the prefix `set`, it's easier to understand what it actually does.

When the `Counter` component renders for the first time, `useState` will return `[0, setCount]`. This is because we passed 0 to `useState` as the initial value for `count`. The `Counter` component will now remember that 0 is the latest state value for `count`.

When we click on the button for the first time, the `increment` method will be called, and it will call `setCount(count + 1)` to update the state of `count` to 1. Remember that `count` is 0, so `setCount(count + 1)` is essentially just (0 + 1). The `Counter` component will now remember

86

that count is 1. Calling setCount(count + 1) also triggers a component re-render. This will be the Counter component's second render.

During the second render, the Counter component will remember that we set count to 1. The useState Hook will return [1, setCount] instead of the [0, setCount] from the first render.

If we keep on clicking the button, count will continue being incremented until the Counter component is unmounted. It can be unmounted if the user navigates away from the page, or if the user closes the browser tab.

If we try re-writing the Counter component above using a local variable instead of state, we'll notice a big difference.

```
const Counter = () => {
  let count: number = 0;

  const increment = () => count + 1;

  return <button onClick={increment}>{count}</button>;
};

export { Counter };
```

Clicking on the button no longer does anything. A button with a label of 0 continues to be displayed on the screen even after clicking it multiple times.

Unlike the useState Hook, the local variable count does not trigger a component re-render with the newly incremented value. The local variable count is not capable of preserving its value between component re-renders. Every time the Counter component re-renders, count will start over at 0.

State is changed only after a re-render

If we try logging `count` to the console immediately after calling `setCount`, we might be surprised by the result.

```
import { useState } from 'react';

const Counter = () => {
  const [count, setCount] = useState<number>(0);

  const increment = () => {
    setCount(count + 1);
    // Bad: won't display the latest `count` value
    console.log(count);
  };

  return <button onClick={increment}>{count}</button>;
};

export { Counter };
```

The first button click will log 0 to the console, but the button will display 1. The second button click will log 1 to the console, but the button will display 2, and so forth.

Rather than logging the `count` value after `count + 1` happens, the previous value is logged to the console. This is because calling the state's setter function, `setCount`, won't change the value for `count` until the `Counter` component re-renders.

By logging to the console immediately after `setCount` is called, we are not waiting for the component to re-render in order to provide us with the updated `count` value. We are instead logging the `count` value that came from the the previous render.

It's important to know that state updates in React are asynchronous. The state's setter function does not actually perform an immediate state update. Instead, it schedules a state update for some unknown time in the future. This means that we can't find out exactly when a state update occurred or will occur, just by looking at the code. The `useState` Hook is asynchronous for performance reasons. This is why state changes don't feel immediate.

Updating state based on the previous state

There are times when it can be helpful to update state using the previous state. Instead of passing a value to the state setter function, we can pass in a function that references the previous state and returns an updated state.

This approach ensures that state updates are based on the previous state, avoiding any race conditions that could arise from multiple state updates happening simultaneously.

Let's update the Counter component's increment method to have it increment the counter by 3 every time.

```
import { useState } from 'react';

const Counter = () => {
  const [count, setCount] = useState<number>(0);

  const increment = () => {
    setCount(count + 1);
    setCount(count + 1);
    setCount(count + 1);
  };

  return <button onClick={increment}>{count}</button>;
};

export { Counter };
```

After one click of the button, count will be 1 instead of 3, even if we called setCount three times. Surprising, right?

This is because, as we saw earlier, calling the state's setter function doesn't update the state variable in the already running code. It only update's the state after the component re-renders. Each call to setCount(count + 1) is just setCount(0 + 1), which is 1, three times in a row!

Instead of passing the next state into setCount, we can pass in an *updater function* that references the previous state. Let's update all three setCount invocations to use the previous state.

```
import { useState } from 'react';

const Counter = () => {
  const [count, setCount] = useState<number>(0);

  const increment = () => {
```

89

```
    setCount(c => c + 1);
    setCount(c => c + 1);
    setCount(c => c + 1);
  };

  return <button onClick={increment}>{count}</button>;
};

export { Counter };
```

In this updated example, `c => c + 1` is our *updater function*. It takes the *pending* state of count and calculates its next state. Where does this pending state come from, you might ask? React puts all our state updater functions in a queue. This queue creates the concept of a pending state.

A queue is a linear data structure. Think of it like a collection of items in which only the earliest added item can be accessed and removed.

When our `Counter` component re-renders, React will execute our updater functions from the queue in the same order that they were added to the queue.

Here is how React will process our updater functions for `setCount` in the queue.

```
// receive 0 as the pending state and return 1 as the next state
c => c + 1
// receive 1 as the pending state and return 2 as the next state
c => c + 1
// receive 2 as the pending state and return 3 as the next state
c => c + 1
```

Once React is done processing the queue containing our updater functions, it will store 3 as the current state for `count`.

It's a common React convention to name the pending state argument using the first letter of the state variable's name, which is c for `count`. This is why we used c as the pending state in our updater function. Some may find it easier to name it `prevCount` or `previousCount`, in order to better understand what it actually represents.

If the state that we are setting needs to be computed from the pending state, we should use the approach outlined here. Using `setCount(c => c + 1)` is a bit more verbose than `setCount(count + 1)`, but it gives us access to the pending state when we need it.

Updating objects and arrays in state

We can use as many state variables as we need in a component. For unrelated state, split it up into separate variables. a component needs to remember a numeric count value as well as a boolean showCount value. The showCount value is for toggling the show or hide status of the count value on the screen. The state of these two is unrelated, so they should be split into two separate state variables.

There are situations where multiple state variables change together. In such cases, it's more convenient to combine these state variables into one object. We'll see this in a later section about managing forms with state in React.

So far, we've only added numbers into state. We can also put objects and arrays into state. The only difference with putting objects and arrays into state is the way that we update them.

In React, state should be treated as *read-only*. We need to replace the state rather than mutate the existing state. This is especially important with objects and arrays.

Updating objects in state

Even if objects in React state can be directly mutated, we should treat them as if they are immutable, or unchangeable - just like numbers, booleans, and strings. Instead of directly mutating objects, we should replace them.

Consider the following UserProfile component that directly mutates an object in state.

```
import { ChangeEvent, useState } from 'react';

type User = {
  firstName: string;
  lastName: string;
};

const UserProfile = () => {
  const [user, setUser] = useState<User>({
    firstName: '',
    lastName: '',
  });

  const handleChange = (e: ChangeEvent<HTMLInputElement>) => {
    // Bad: direct state mutation
    user[e.target.name as keyof User] = e.target.value;
  }
```

```
  return (
    <>
      <label>
        First name:
        <input
          name="firstName"
          value={user.firstName}
          onChange={handleChange}
        />
      </label>
      <label>
        Last name:
        <input
          name="lastName"
          value={user.lastName}
          onChange={handleChange}
        />
      </label>
      <p>
        {user.firstName}{' '}
        {user.lastName}
      </p>
    </>
  );
};

export { UserProfile };
```

In the `UserProfile` component above, we directly mutated the `user` state object within the `handleChange` event handler function. As a result, typing into the form fields for "First Name" and "Last Name" doesn't do anything. We're unable to add any values to the two input fields.

The two input fields don't work because the `handleChange` event handler directly mutates the `user` state. We can fix this issue by replacing the state object for `user` rather than directly mutating it.

```
const handleChange = (e: ChangeEvent<HTMLInputElement>) => {
  // Good: state replaced with a new object
  setUser({
    ...user,
    [e.target.name]: e.target.value
  });
};
```

With this change, the form fields work properly. Typing in a first name and last name into the input fields renders them to the screen, right below the form.

When handleChange is called, setUser replaces the user state with a new object. Only one of the form fields is updated at a time. As a result, we need to preserve the value of the other form field. This is why we used the spread syntax on the user object (...user) when creating the new object. The spread syntax copies all of an object's property-value pairs rather than having to type them out manually.

After copying the user object into the new object, we overwrite the value of the object property that needs to be changed. If the firstName field is being updated, then e.target.name will be firstName, and e.target.value will be the value of that field. The same goes for the lastName field.

Notice that we didn't declare separate state variables for firstName and lastName. We grouped all the form data in the same object. It's more convenient to manage form state this way. However, updating an object in state is not as straightforward, so we must be careful to do it properly.

Updating nested state objects

Let's take a look at how to properly update objects in state when they are nested more than one level deep.

```
const [user, setUser] = useState({
  firstName: 'John',
  lastName: 'Smith',
  location: {
    city: 'Montreal',
    province: 'Quebec',
    country: 'Canada',
  },
});
```

Let's say that we want to update the value for city in the user state object. It's two levels deep. How can we do it? Remember, we don't want to do it by direct mutation, like this.

```
user.location.city = 'Quebec City';
```

Let's do it the right way. In order to update the nested city property, we'll need to first create a new location object, pre-populate it with data from the current location object, and overwrite the city. Then, we'll need to create a new user object, pre-populate it with data from the current user object, and overwrite the location with the new location object. Here's what this would look like if we did it step-by-step.

```
const newLocation = { ...user.location, city: 'Quebec City' };
const newUser = { ...user, location: newLocation };
setUser(newUser);
```

Any mutations made to the newLocation and newUser objects would be fine here because we'd be mutating objects that we just created. No other code references these objects yet, so we are free to mutate them. Such mutations would be called *local mutations*. Mutations are problematic only when they change objects that are already placed in state.

We can also write the code above as a single call to the setUser state setter function.

```
setUser({
  ...user, // Copy other user fields
  location: { // but replace the location
    ...user.location, // copy other location fields
    city: 'Quebec City' // but replace the city
  },
});
```

Here's what this would look like in a UserProfile component.

```
import { ChangeEvent, useState } from 'react';

const UserProfile = () => {
  const [user, setUser] = useState({
    firstName: 'John',
    lastName: 'Smith',
    location: {
      city: 'Montreal',
      province: 'Quebec',
      country: 'Canada',
    },
  });

  // Good: state replaced with a new object
  const handleChange = (e: ChangeEvent<HTMLInputElement>) => {
    setUser({
      ...user, // Copy other user fields
      location: { // but replace the location
        ...user.location, // copy other location fields
        city: e.target.value, // but replace the city
      },
    });
  };

  return (
    <>
      <label>
```

```
          City:
          <input
            name="city"
            value={user.location.city}
            onChange={handleChange}
          />
        </label>
        <p>
          City: {user.location.city}
        </p>
      </>
  );
};

export { UserProfile };
```

Adding to an array in state

Let's look at how we can add an item to an array in state. We will create a new array that contains all the existing items, plus a new item at the end. The simplest way to do this is to use the JavaScript spread operator.

Consider the following `ProductList` component that allows us to add new products to a list of products.

```
import { useState } from 'react';

type Product = {
  id: number;
  name: string;
  price: number;
}

const productList: Product[] = [
  { id: 1, name: 'PlayStation 5', price: 500 },
  { id: 2, name: 'TV', price: 1500 },
  { id: 3, name: 'Speakers', price: 750 },
];

const ProductList = () => {
  const [name, setName] = useState<string>('');
  const [price, setPrice] = useState<string>('');
  const [products, setProducts] = useState<Product[]>(productList);

  const handleAdd = () => {
    setName('');
    setPrice('');
    setProducts([
```

```
        ...products,
        {
          id: products[products.length - 1].id + 1,
          name,
          price: parseInt(price),
        },
      ]);
    };

    return (
      <>
        <div>
          <h4>Add Product</h4>
          <input
            type="text"
            value={name}
            placeholder="Product name..."
            onChange={e => setName(e.target.value)}
          />
          <input
            type="text"
            value={price}
            placeholder="Product price..."
            onChange={e => setPrice(e.target.value)}
          />
          <button onClick={handleAdd}>Add Product</button>
        </div>

        <h4>Products</h4>
        <ul>
          {products.map(({ id, name, price }) => (
            <li key={id}>
              {name}, $ {price}
            </li>
          ))}
        </ul>
      </>
    );
};

export { ProductList };
```

Every time we make a change to the product name field, it will save the value in state using the setName state setter function. Then, the state variable name will contain the value that we last typed into the input field. The same goes for the price field.

When we click on "Add Product", the `handleAdd` event handler function is called. It clears the name stored in state using `setName('')` so that the input field is cleared. This will allow us to keep adding more products. The `price` field is also cleared.

Next, a new array is created within the `setProducts` state setter function. Existing products are copied into the new array using the JavaScript spread operator. The new product is then added as an object at the end of the new array. The `setProducts` state setter function then re-renders the component with the new array as the value for the `products` state.

After typing in a new product name and price, and then clicking on the "Add Product" button, the list of products displayed on the screen is updated to show our new product.

Deleting from an array in state

To delete an element from an array without mutating it directly, we can use the JavaScript array `filter` method. This method does not modify the original array. Instead, it will produce a new array that does not contain the element that we want to remove.

Let's update the `ProductList` component to make it possible to delete products from state.

```
import { useState } from 'react';

type Product = {
  id: number;
  name: string;
  price: number;
}

const productList: Product[] = [
  { id: 1, name: 'PlayStation 5', price: 500 },
  { id: 2, name: 'TV', price: 1500 },
  { id: 3, name: 'Speakers', price: 750 },
];

const ProductList = () => {
  const [name, setName] = useState<string>('');
  const [price, setPrice] = useState<string>('');
  const [products, setProducts] = useState<Product[]>(productList);

  const handleAdd = () => {
    setName('');
    setPrice('');
    setProducts([
      ...products,
```

```
      {
        id: products[products.length - 1].id + 1,
        name,
        price: parseInt(price),
      },
    ]);
  };

  const handleDelete = (productToDelete: string) => {
    const updatedProducts = products.filter(product => product.name !== produ
ctToDelete);
    setProducts(updatedProducts);
  };

  return (
    <>
      <div>
        <h4>Add Product</h4>
        <input
          type="text"
          value={name}
          placeholder="Product name..."
          onChange={e => setName(e.target.value)}
        />
        <input
          type="text"
          value={price}
          placeholder="Product price..."
          onChange={e => setPrice(e.target.value)}
        />
        <button onClick={handleAdd}>Add Product</button>
      </div>

      <h4>Products</h4>
      <ul>
        {products.map(({ id, name, price }) => (
          <li key={id}>
            {name}, $ {price} <button onClick={() => handleDelete(name)}>Dele
te</button>
          </li>
        ))}
      </ul>
    </>
  );
};

export { ProductList };
```

We added a "Delete" button beside every product in the list. Clicking on a "Delete" button calls the `handleDelete` event handler, passing it the name of the product to delete. The array `filter` method filters out the product that was selected for deletion from the `products` state. It then returns a new array without the deleted product. Then, the state setter function `setProducts` saves this new array to the `products` state and triggers a component re-render.

If we try clicking on the "Delete" button beside any product, that product will no longer be displayed in the list of products.

Updating an array in state

In JavaScript, arrays are mutable but we should treat them as immutable when we store them in state - just like we did with objects earlier.

When we need to update an array stored in state, we should create a new array and then set save this new array in state.

We should avoid using methods that mutate an array, such as `push`, `pop`, and `splice`. We should instead create a new array from the original array in state by using non-mutating methods, such as `filter`, `map`, and `slice`. These non-mutating methods will return a new array that we can then save in state. If we need to sort an array that's in state, we should first copy that array, sort it, and then set the copied-and-sorted array using the state setter function.

Let's update the `ProductList` component we saw earlier to update an array item in state. We want to be able to lower the price of only the "PlayStation 5" product by $50 dollars, as long as its current price is not lower than $100.

```
import { useState } from 'react';

type Product = {
  id: number;
  name: string;
  price: number;
}

const productList: Product[] = [
  { id: 1, name: 'PlayStation 5', price: 500 },
  { id: 2, name: 'TV', price: 1500 },
  { id: 3, name: 'Speakers', price: 750 },
];
```

```
const ProductList = () => {
  const [name, setName] = useState<string>('');
  const [price, setPrice] = useState<string>('');
  const [products, setProducts] = useState<Product[]>(productList);

  const handleAdd = () => {
    setName('');
    setPrice('');
    setProducts([
      ...products,
      {
        id: products[products.length - 1].id + 1,
        name,
        price: parseInt(price),
      },
    ]);
  };

  const handleDelete = (productToDelete: string) => {
    const updatedProducts = products.filter(product => product.name !== productToDelete);
    setProducts(updatedProducts);
  };

  const handleDiscount = () => {
    const updatedProducts = products.map((product) => {
      if (product.name === 'PlayStation 5' && product.price > 100) {
        // Return a new product
        return {
          ...product,
          price: product.price - 50,
        };
      } else {
        // No change
        return product;
      }
    });
    // re-render with the updated array
    setProducts(updatedProducts);
  };

  return (
    <>
      <div>
        <h4>Add Product</h4>
        <input
          type="text"
          value={name}
          placeholder="Product name..."
          onChange={e => setName(e.target.value)}
```

```jsx
      />
      <input
        type="text"
        value={price}
        placeholder="Product price..."
        onChange={e => setPrice(e.target.value)}
      />
      <button onClick={handleAdd}>Add Product</button>
    </div>

    <div>
      <h4>Discounts</h4>
      <button onClick={handleDiscount}>PlayStation 5 Discount</button>
    </div>

    <h4>Products</h4>
    <ul>
      {products.map(({ id, name, price }) => (
        <li key={id}>
          {name}, $ {price} <button onClick={() => handleDelete(name)}>Delete</button>
        </li>
      ))}
    </ul>
  </>
  );
};

export { ProductList };
```

Clicking on the "PlayStation 5 Discount" button lowers the price of the "PlayStation 5" product by $50 dollars, as long as its current price is not lower than $100. No other product prices are affected.

Clicking on the "PlayStation 5 Discount" button calls the `handleDiscount` event handler function. Within this function, the `map` method is used to iterate over the `products` in state. While iterating over the array of `products`, we searched for the matching product to discount, copied that product's details into a new object using the JavaScript spread operator, set a discounted price for it, and then returned the new object. The `map` method returned a new array containing a new object for only the discounted product. This new array was then passed in to the `setProducts` state setter function in order to update the `products` state and re-render the component.

useState and child components

We learned that React triggers a component re-render whenever the setter function of the useState hook is called. This doesn't only mean that the component itself will re-render. It also means that any child components contained within this component will also re-render.

Child components will re-render when their parent component re-renders, regardless of whether their own props have changed or not. To illustrate this, consider the following example where we split the Counter component into a CounterChanger parent component and a CounterDisplay child component.

```
import { useState } from "react";

type Props = {
  counter: number;
};

const CounterDisplay = ({ counter }: Props) => {
  return (
    <p>{counter}</p>
  );
}

const CounterChanger = () => {
  const [value, setValue] = useState(0);

  return (
    <div>
      <CounterDisplay counter={value} />
      <button onClick={() => setValue(Math.random())}>Change Value</button>
    </div>
  );
};

export { CounterChanger };
```

The CounterDisplay component doesn't need to use any state. This is because it will automatically re-render when its parent component, CounterChanger re-renders.

The CounterDisplay component is a *dumb* component, or a *presentation* component. It contains no state and no internal business logic. It's only responsibility is to present (or display) something. It's a very reusable component. On the other hand, CounterChanger is a *smart* or *stateful* component because it contains state-related logic.

The CounterChanger component re-renders every time the "Change Value" button is pressed. This is because each button press calls the `setValue` state setter function, which updates the state for `value` and re-renders the component to reflect the updated `value`. The updated `value` is then passed along to the CounterDisplay component via its props, where it gets displayed to the screen.

Always keep in mind that child components re-render whenever their parent component re-renders. This important detail must be considered when designing the component architecture for our applications. If we build a poorly structured component architecture, or if we are not careful with our placement of component state, we could end up unnecessarily re-rendering many child components that don't actually need to be re-rendered. This can create a performance bottleneck in our application.

When initial state is expensive

When it comes to initial state, React saves it once, when the component first renders, and then ignores it when the component re-renders. When the initialization of our state is computationally expensive, we must be careful how we define that initial state, or it can create performance issues.

Let's take a look at the following example of a `Cart` component that needs its `product` state to be initialized by a computationally expensive operation. To simulate a computationally expensive operation, we'll fetch the current `product` from local storage. In order to do so, a product needs to be in local storage, so we'll set one up for demonstration purposes.

```
import { useState } from "react";

type Product = {
  id: number;
  name: string;
  price: number;
}

// set data in localStorage
// for the initializer function to fetch
localStorage.setItem('product', JSON.stringify({
  id: 1,
  name: "Logitech mouse",
  price: 100,
}));

const Cart = () => {
  const getInitialState = (): Product | null => {
    console.log('getInitialState() called...');
```

```
    const product = localStorage.getItem('product');

    if (product) {
      return JSON.parse(product);
    }
    return null;
  };

  // Bad: initializer function will be called on every render
  const [product, setProduct] = useState<Product | null>(getInitialState());

  const updateState = () => {
    setProduct({
      id: 1,
      name: "Logitech mouse",
      price: 100,
    });
  }

  if (!product) {
    return <p>Product not found.</p>
  }

  return (
    <>
      <p>{product.name}, ${product.price}</p>
      <button onClick={updateState}>Update state</button>
    </>
  );
};

export { Cart };
```

Using getInitialState() within useState will call the function on every component render and pass the result of calling the function to useState. This can be a waste of resources if the function is handling a lot of data or performing expensive calculations.

When we click on the "Update state" button, a bogus component re-render will be triggered for demonstration purposes. We'll notice that the console.log statement within the getInitialState function gets logged to the console for each component re-render. This is not what we want. We want to initialize state once, on the initial render of the component, not on every render.

```
// Good: initializer function only called on the first render
const [product, setProduct] = useState<Product | null>(getInitialState);
```

Instead, when we use `getInitialState` within `useState`, we are passing the function itself rather than the result of calling the function. When we pass the function itself, it will only be called once, during the first render of the component. This is how a true *lazy initializer* function works.

If we comment out the *Bad* line of code and replace it with the *Good* line of code, the `console.log` statement within the `getInitialState` function will only get logged to the console during the initial component render. This is exactly what we want.

This approach should only be used for computationally expensive state initialization that we don't want running on every component render. We shouldn't use *lazy initialization* everywhere. Lazy initialization is not a technique that is used often, but when we do need it, it will help us avoid a potential performance bottleneck.

If the `getInitialState` function needs to receive arguments, we can still write it as a *lazy initializer* function for `useState`. Here's what it would look like.

```
import { useState } from "react";

type Product = {
  id: number;
  name: string;
  price: number;
}

type Props = {
  userId: number;
};

const getInitialState = (userId: number): Product | null => {
  console.log('getInitialState() called...');

  // ...
};

const Cart = ({ userId }: Props) => {
  const [product, setProduct] = useState<Product>(() => getInitialState(userId));

  // ...
};

export { Cart }
```

105

The lazy initializer function doesn't have to be present within the component. In this example, we moved the `getInitialState` function outside of the component.

We used an anonymous function (a function without a name) within `useState` to call the `getInitialState` lazy initializer function for us with the `userId` argument. This anonymous function then returns its result to `useState` so that it can be used to initialize the `product` state.

If we had used `getInitialState(userId)` within `useState`, without the anonymous function, we would have been assigning the result of calling the function rather than the function itself. The function would get called on every component render rather than only on the initial render.

useState with one element

The `useState` Hook returns an array with two elements, the state variable and a state setter function to update the state variable.

We usually need both elements together to manage state. However, there may be times that we only need one of the two elements. To use `useState` with just one of the two elements, we can ignore the unused element.

If we only need the state variable, we can ignore the state setter function, like this:

```
const [stateVariable] = useState(initialState);
```

If we only need the state setter function, we can ignore the state variable, like this:

```
const [, stateSetterFunction] = useState(initialState);
```

useState recap

- State variables are declared using the `useState` Hook.
- Use a state variable when a component needs to *remember* information between renders.
- The `useState` Hook returns an array of two values: the current state and the function that updates it.
- More than one state variable can be defined in a component.
- A re-render triggered by `useState` in a parent component re-renders all of its child components.
- When a computationally expensive operation is needed to initialize state, consider using a lazy initializer function.

State strategies

Let's consider strategies for how to best use state within React components. We'll learn how to *lift state* and how to *colocate state*.

Before diving into strategies for component state, we first need to know that state is private. The state that we define in a component is *local* to a single component instance on the screen. If we render the same component to the screen two times, each copy of that component will have it's own isolated state, separate from the other. If we change the state of one component, that change will not be reflected in the other component.

Let's take a look at an example of an App component that renders two Counter components.

```
import { useState } from 'react';

const Counter = () => {
  const [count, setCount] = useState<number>(0);

  const increment = () => setCount(count + 1);

  return <button onClick={increment}>{count}</button>
};

const App = () => {
  return (
    <>
      <Counter />
      <Counter />
    </>
  );
};

export { App };
```

The state of each Counter component is stored separately. Clicking on the button of one Counter only increments the value displayed by that Counter instance. The newly incremented value does not get reflected in the other Counter component displayed beside it.

The parent component, App, knows nothing about the state in its children. State is private to the component that uses it. This allows us to add or remove state from a component without impacting any other components.

What if we encounter a scenario where multiple child components need to have their states in sync? This is where *lifting state* comes in handy.

Lifting State

Lifting state is the process of moving a component's state higher up the component tree to its parent component. Lifting state up is used when multiple components need to share the same data.

When a sibling component needs the state that's living in another one of its siblings, the solution is to lift that state upward. That state needs to be lifted out from the sibling component and inserted into the closest shared parent component. This parent component is the parent of both siblings, so it can easily share its state with both siblings. The way that the parent component shares its state is by passing it as props to the children components that need it.

This process is called lifting state because we're taking state that's lower down in the component tree and lifting it up to the common parent that's higher up in the component tree.

Let's take a look at an example of lifting state. In this example, a `Name` component will prompt the user for their name, a `FavoriteMovie` component will prompt the user for their favorite movie, and a `Greeting` component will greet the user by name.

```
import { ChangeEvent, useState } from 'react';

type NameProps = {
  name: string;
  onChange: (event: ChangeEvent<HTMLInputElement>) => void;
}

const Name = ({ name, onChange }: NameProps) => {
  return (
    <div>
      <label htmlFor="name">Name</label>
      <input id="name" value={name} onChange={onChange} />
    </div>
  );
};

const FavoriteMovie = () => {
  const [movie, setMovie] = useState<string>('');

  return (
    <div>
      <label htmlFor="movie">Favorite Movie</label>
```

```
      <input
        id="movie"
        value={movie}
        onChange={event => setMovie(event.target.value)}
      />
    </div>
  );
}

type GreetingProps = {
  name: string;
}

const Greeting = ({ name }: GreetingProps) => {
  return <p>Hello, {name}.</p>
}

const App = () => {
  const [name, setName] = useState<string>('');

  return (
    <form>
      <Name name={name} onChange={event => setName(event.target.value)} />
      <FavoriteMovie />
      <Greeting name={name} />
    </form>
  );
};

export { App };
```

In the example above, the `movie` state is local to the `FavoriteMovie` component. This becomes a problem if we want the `Greeting` component to display the user's favorite movie alongside their name. How could we give the `Greeting` component access to the `movie` state?

The best way would be to lift the `movie` state up to the `App` component, and then to pass the `movie` state as a prop to the `FavoriteMovie` and `Greeting` components. Lifting the `movie` state to the `App` component is ideal because it is the closest parent component that has both `FavoriteMovie` and `Greeting` as child components.

Let's go ahead and update the example above by lifting the `movie` state up to the `App` component.

```
import { ChangeEvent, useState } from 'react';

type NameProps = {
```

```
  name: string;
  onChange: (event: ChangeEvent<HTMLInputElement>) => void;
}

const Name = ({ name, onChange }: NameProps) => {
  return (
    <div>
      <label htmlFor="name">Name</label>
      <input id="name" value={name} onChange={onChange} />
    </div>
  );
};

type FavoriteMovieProps = {
  movie: string;
  onChange: (event: ChangeEvent<HTMLInputElement>) => void;
}

const FavoriteMovie = ({ movie, onChange }: FavoriteMovieProps) => {
  return (
    <div>
      <label htmlFor="movie">Favorite Movie</label>
      <input id="movie" value={movie} onChange={onChange} />
    </div>
  );
};

type GreetingProps = {
  name: string;
  movie: string;
};

const Greeting = ({ name, movie }: GreetingProps) => {
  return (
    <p>
      Hello, {name}. Your favorite movie is {movie}.
    </p>
  );
};

const App = () => {
  const [name, setName] = useState<string>('');
  const [movie, setMovie] = useState<string>('');

  return (
    <form>
      <Name name={name} onChange={event => setName(event.target.value)} />
      <FavoriteMovie movie={movie} onChange={event => setMovie(event.target.value)} />
      <Greeting name={name} movie={movie} />
```

```
        </form>
    );
}

export { App };
```

After lifting the `movie` state to the `App` component, we can now pass the `movie` state as props to the child components that need it. We updated both the `FavoriteMovie` and `Greeting` components to receive a `movie` prop. We also updated the `Greeting` component to display the user's favorite movie.

The next step was to hook up the setter method for updating the `movie` state, which is now in the `App` component. To do this, we added an `onChange` prop to `FavoriteMovie` that receives an event handler function. We then updated the `onChange` event on the favorite movie text box so that it calls the event handler function received via the `onChange` prop. This was necessary because the `movie` state's `setMovie` setter method is now in the `App` component, not in the `FavoriteMovie` component.

The *lifting state* refactor is now complete. The `Greeting` and `FavoriteMovie` components are now both making use of the `movie` state that was lifted to their parent component, `App`. We lifted state so that more than one component can make use of that state in the most optimal way.

Colocating state

Colocating state means putting state as close to where it's being used. The goal is to push state down in order to keep it closest to the components that actually use it. We should avoid global state unless we absolutely need it, and aim to colocate state instead.

Let's practice colocating state by revisiting the previous example, consisting of the `FavoriteMovie` and `Greeting` components. Let's pretend we received a requirement change request for the `Greeting` component. The `Greeting` component must now only display the user's favorite movie, and not their name.

Let's update the `Greeting` component to simply receive the `movie` prop and remove references to the `name` prop. This can easily be done. However, every time we refactor components, we should also look for opportunities to colocate state.

```
import { ChangeEvent, useState } from 'react';
```

```
type NameProps = {
  name: string;
  onChange: (event: ChangeEvent<HTMLInputElement>) => void;
};

const Name = ({ name, onChange }: NameProps) => {
  return (
    <div>
      <label htmlFor="name">Name</label>
      <input id="name" value={name} onChange={onChange} />
    </div>
  );
};

type FavoriteMovieProps = {
  movie: string;
  onChange: (event: ChangeEvent<HTMLInputElement>) => void;
};

const FavoriteMovie = ({ movie, onChange }: FavoriteMovieProps) => {
  return (
    <div>
      <label htmlFor="movie">Favorite Movie</label>
      <input
        id="movie"
        value={movie}
        onChange={onChange}
      />
    </div>
  );
};

type GreetingProps = {
  movie: string;
};

const Greeting = ({ movie }: GreetingProps) => {
  return <p>Your favorite movie is {movie}.</p>
};

const App = () => {
  const [name, setName] = useState<string>('');
  const [movie, setMovie] = useState<string>('');

  return (
    <form>
      <Name name={name} onChange={event => setName(event.target.value)} />
      <FavoriteMovie movie={movie} onChange={event => setMovie(event.target.value)} />
      <Greeting movie={movie} />
```

```
      </form>
  );
};

export { App };
```

After removing references to the name prop from the Greeting component, we'll notice a good opportunity to colocate state. The state for name is still defined in the App component, but it's now only used in the Name component. We should move the state for name closer to the component(s) that actually use it. This will make our code more maintainable. It can even end up making our code more performant.

After our change to the Greeting component, the Name component is the only one that needs the name state. Therefore, let's push the name state down from the App component to the Name component.

```
import { ChangeEvent, useState } from 'react';

const Name = () => {
  const [name, setName] = useState<string>('');

  return (
    <div>
      <label htmlFor="name">Name</label>
      <input id="name" value={name} onChange={event => setName(event.target.value)} />
    </div>
  );
};

type FavoriteMovieProps = {
  movie: string;
  onChange: (event: ChangeEvent<HTMLInputElement>) => void;
};

const FavoriteMovie = ({ movie, onChange }: FavoriteMovieProps) => {
  return (
    <div>
      <label htmlFor="movie">Favorite Movie</label>
      <input id="movie" value={movie} onChange={onChange} />
    </div>
  );
};

type GreetingProps = {
  movie: string;
```

```
};

const Greeting = ({ movie }: GreetingProps) => {
  return <p>Your favorite movie is {movie}.</p>
};

const App = () => {
  const [movie, setMovie] = useState<string>('');

  return (
    <form>
      <Name />
      <FavoriteMovie movie={movie} onChange={event => setMovie(event.target.value)} />
      <Greeting movie={movie} />
    </form>
  );
};

export { App };
```

We removed the name and onChange props from the Name component. We no longer need these props because the name state is now local to the Name component.

Then, we hooked up the setter method for updating the name state. We updated the onChange event on the name's text box so that it calls setName directly. Since the name state's setter method now lives in the Name component, we can make direct use of it.

Moving the name state from the App to the Name component is what's referred to as *state colocation*. By using state colocation, we achieved two benefits.

- **Organized code that separates concerns:** We don't have to be concerned with the name state when maintaining the App component.
- **More performant code:** The performance gain comes from the fact that the App component no longer needs to be re-rendered every time the name state is updated. Only the Name component will be re-rendered when the name state is updated. The name state will be updated every time the name's text box is changed, thereby calling setName, which triggers a component re-render.

State strategies recap

- State is private. The state in a component is local to a single component instance on the screen.
- Lifting state means moving state up from a child component to the closest parent, so that it can be shared across multiple sibling components. Lifting state is useful when sibling components need to know about a common state.
- State colocation means pushing state down, thus, closer to the component(s) that actually need it. Colocating state results in code that is more maintainable and more performant.
- Lifting state and colocating state are two techniques that help us use state more effectively across our component tree.

The useReducer hook

The React `useReducer` Hook is an alternative to the `useState` Hook. The `useReducer` Hook is a better option than the `useState` Hook when dealing with complex state logic. For those familiar with **Redux** (https://redux.js.org), using the `useReducer` Hook is similar to using *reducers* in Redux.

Declaring the useReducer Hook

```
const [state, dispatch] = useReducer(reducer, initialState);
```

The `useReducer` hook receives two arguments:

- **A reducer:** A pure function that updates the state in an immutable way and returns the new state.
- **An initial state:** The initial value of the state that we want to start with.

Similar to the `useState` Hook, the `useReducer` Hook returns an array of two elements:

- **The current state:** In the example above, it's called `state`.
- **A dispatch function:** A special function that dispatches the action to perform on the state. In the example above, the dispatch function is simply called `dispatch`.

Using the useReducer hook

The `useReducer` Hook is commonly used to manage complex state using an object. However, to start with a very simple example, let's begin by using the `useReducer` Hook to manage the numeric state of a counter.

```
import { useReducer } from 'react';

const counterReducer = (state: number, action: number) => state + action;

const Counter = () => {
  const [state, dispatch] = useReducer(counterReducer, 0);

  const increment = () => dispatch(1);

  return <button onClick={increment}>{state}</button>;
};

export { Counter };
```

The first render of the Counter component will create the state via the useReducer Hook, and that state will persist across component re-renders.

The name of the *reducer* function that we defined is counterReducer. We passed it as the first parameter of useReducer. We then defined an initial state of 0 using the second parameter of useReducer.

The useReducer hook returns an array containing the state, which we defined as a number in the counterReducer function, and it also returns the dispatch function to update the state. The dispatch function receives a number since we defined action to be of type number in the counterReducer function.

Clicking on the button dispatches an action with a value of 1 that gets added to the current state within the counterReducer function. The component then re-renders and displays the new state.

When making use of the Counter component, we'll see the label of the button displaying 0. The button label will increase by 1 with every click of the button.

useReducer with objects

Let's now look at how the useReducer Hook is most commonly implemented, with state as an object. This common way of using useReducer is inspired by the Redux state management library.

Let's start by creating a counterReducer.ts file for our reducer function. Then, let's define a counterReducer function within it.

```
type CounterState = {
  count: number;
}

enum CounterActionType {
  Increment = 'INCREMENT',
}

type CounterAction = {
  type: CounterActionType;
  payload: number;
}

const initialCounterState: CounterState = {
  count: 0,
};
```

```
const counterReducer = (state: CounterState, action: CounterAction) => {
  const { type, payload } = action;

  switch (type) {
    case CounterActionType.Increment: {
      return {
        ...state,
        count: state.count + payload,
      };
    }
    default: {
      return state;
    }
  }
};

export { counterReducer, initialCounterState, CounterActionType };
```

The counterReducer.ts file exports the reducer function, counterReducer, as well as the initial state, initialCounterState. Both are needed to initialize the useReducer Hook in a component. This file also exports the CounterActionType so that we can use it to identify the actions that we want to dispatch from the component.

Here's an overview of the types that we created in the above file for our reducer function.

- CounterState is the type definition for our counter's state.
- CounterActionType is a TypeScript enum containing string identifiers for the different action types that we want to support.
- CounterAction is the type definition for the actions that will be triggered by the dispatch function provided by useReducer.

We defined the counterReducer function to take two arguments, state and action. We destructured the action object to get the type and payload from it. We then used a switch statement on the type property to check for different action types so that we can update our state based on the action performed.

In this simple example, we have only one action type, increment. However, we could have had others, such as decrement, to decrement the counter.

Notice that within the case statement for CounterActionType.Increment, we updated the state in an immutable way. We copied the state to a new object with the spread operator and then updated the value for count.

Why did we do this? Remember that a reducer is a pure function, which means that it should not directly modify the state. Instead, it should create and return a new object representing the updated state. Avoid mutating the state object directly from within a reducer function in order to prevent unexpected results.

Let's now make use of counterReducer.ts within a Counter component that we will define in a Counter.tsx file.

```
import { useReducer } from 'react';
import { counterReducer, initialCounterState, CounterActionType } from './cou
nterReducer';

const Counter = () => {
  const [state, dispatch] = useReducer(counterReducer, initialCounterState);

  const increment = () => dispatch({ type: CounterActionType.Increment, paylo
ad: 1 });

  return <button onClick={increment}>{state.count}</button>;
};

export { Counter };
```

We imported counterReducer and initialCounterState from the reducer's file and used them to initialize the useReducer hook. We also imported CounterActionType and used it to specify the type of the action object being dispatched when the button is clicked.

The increment event handler function calls the dispatch method provided by useReducer. We passed an object to the dispatch call. This object is called an *action object*.

An action object is an object that is used to describe how the state should be updated. An action object usually has a property named type, which is used to identify what kind of operation the reducer must perform.

We passed CounterActionType.Increment to the action object's type property because we want to increment the counter. We then specified the value with which to increment the counter using the action object's payload property.

An advantage to using the CounterActionType enum, compared to just using a string value such as "increment", is that no typos will be permitted for the action object's type. The Visual Studio Code IntelliSense will flag any spelling mistakes when referring to a TypeScript enum. If we use a string, we could easily misspell the string value for the action type, either in the dispatch method or in the reducer, and end up with a reducer that doesn't work.

Multiple action types

Let's add another action type to the previous example, called decrement, which will decrement the state of the counter. First, let's update the counterReducer.ts file.

```
type CounterState = {
  count: number;
}

enum CounterActionType {
  Increment = 'INCREMENT',
  Decrement = 'DECREMENT',
}

type CounterAction = {
  type: CounterActionType;
  payload: number;
}

const initialCounterState: CounterState = {
  count: 0,
};

const counterReducer = (state: CounterState, action: CounterAction) => {
  const { type, payload } = action;
  switch (type) {
    case CounterActionType.Increment: {
      return {
        ...state,
        count: state.count + payload,
      };
    }
    case CounterActionType.Decrement: {
      return {
        ...state,
```

```
        count: state.count - payload,
      };
    }
    default: {
      return state;
    }
  }
};

export { counterReducer, initialCounterState, CounterActionType };
```

We added Decrement to the CounterActionType enum and added a case for the CounterActionType.Decrement action type within counterReducer. For the decrement case, we subtract from the count value rather than adding to it.

Let's now update the Counter component to use the new action type that we just created.

```
import { useReducer } from 'react';
import { counterReducer, initialCounterState, CounterActionType } from './cou
nterReducer';

const Counter = () => {
  const [state, dispatch] = useReducer(counterReducer, initialCounterState);

  const increment = () => dispatch({ type: CounterActionType.Increment, paylo
ad: 1 });
  const decrement = () => dispatch({ type: CounterActionType.Decrement, paylo
ad: 1 });

  return (
    <>
      <p>{state.count}</p>
      <button onClick={increment}>Increment</button>
      <button onClick={decrement}>Decrement</button>
    </>
  );
};

export { Counter };
```

We created two new buttons for incrementing and decrementing our counter. We added a decrement event handler function for the onClick event of the "Decrement" button. This event handler dispatches an action to decrement the counter state by 1.

Clicking on either button will dispatch the corresponding action type. We can now see the counter increase or decrease in value depending on the button clicked.

Lazy initialization with useReducer

We pass a function as the third argument to the `useReducer` Hook. The function will be used for *lazy initialization*. The `useReducer` Hook passes its second argument, the initial state, to the lazy initializer function, and then uses the value returned by this function as the actual initial state.

The lazy initializer function can be useful if we need to perform some expensive operation to initialize our state. Examples of expensive operations could include reading from local storage or fetching data asynchronously from an API.

We want to avoid running expensive operations on every component re-render. The solution to that is the lazy initializer function, which will only run once.

Let's see what lazy initialization looks like when applied to the `useReducer` Hook for our `Counter` component.

Firstly, let's add a type export from `counterReducer.ts` so that we can make use of the type `CounterState` for the lazy initializer function in this example.

```
export type { CounterState };
```

Now, let's update the `Counter` component to use a lazy initializer function, named `counterInitializer`, as the third parameter of the `useReducer` Hook.

```
import { useReducer } from 'react';
import { counterReducer, initialCounterState, CounterState, CounterActionType
} from './counterReducer';

const Counter = () => {
  const counterInitializer = (initialState: CounterState) => {
    localStorage.setItem('count', '12');

    const localStorageCount = localStorage.getItem('count');
    const count = localStorageCount ? parseInt(localStorageCount) : 0;

    return {
      count: initialState.count + count,
    };
  };

  const [state, dispatch] = useReducer(
    counterReducer,
    initialCounterState,
    counterInitializer,
```

```
  );
  const increment = () => dispatch({ type: CounterActionType.Increment, paylo
ad: 1 });
  return <button onClick={increment}>{state.count}</button>;
};
export { Counter }
```

The counterInitializer function is our lazy initializer function. In this function, we read a count value from local storage, and then add that value to the count value of 0 from initialCounterState.

In order to simulate that a specific count value exists in local storage, we set it to 12, right before reading it from local storage.

When running this example, we see that the state for the count value now starts at 12 rather than 0. The lazy initializer function transforms the initial state object of { count: 0 }, creating a new initial state of { count: 12 }.

useReducer versus useState

Don't just switch from useState to useReducer when you notice a growing number of useState declarations in a component. We must consider more than that when deciding on which state-related Hook to use.

We should use the useState Hook to manage independent elements of state that do not depend on other state elements. We should use the useReducer Hook to manage elements of state that need to be changed or updated together.

Consider a shopping cart example. When the items in a shopping cart are updated, the total price needs to also be updated. Thus, the cart's total price depends on the cart's items in order to be updated. In this case, it's a good idea to use useReducer instead of useState for managing the cart's state.

A good rule of thumb is to start with useState and only move to useReducer when you start noticing dependencies between state elements. When one state element relies on the value of another state element in order to be updated properly, switch to useReducer.

useReducer to manage dependent state elements

Let's see how we can use the `useReducer` Hook for a more realistic scenario, one where there's elements of state that need to be updated together.

A good example of this is a form with a `country` field and a `city` field. The values of both fields will be elements of state and they will need to be updated together.

When the user changes `country` value, the `city` value in state should be reset. The change in `country` must invalidate any `city` value that was stored in state. This is because every country has it's own list of cities. When the `country` selection changes, so must the `city`.

Let's begin by creating a `formReducer.ts` file. We can grab the code that we used above for the `counterReducer` and change it so that it supports a state with `country` and `city` values.

```
type FormState = {
  country: string;
  city: string;
};

enum FormActionType {
  ChangeCountry = 'ChangeCountry',
  ChangeCity = 'ChangeCity',
}

type FormAction = {
  type: FormActionType;
  payload: string;
};

const initialFormState: FormState = {
  country: '',
  city: '',
};

const formReducer = (state: FormState, action: FormAction): FormState => {
  const { type, payload } = action;

  switch (type) {
    case FormActionType.ChangeCountry: {
      return {
        ...state,
        country: payload,
        city: '',
      };
    }
```

```
    case FormActionType.ChangeCity: {
      return {
        ...state,
        city: payload,
      };
    }
    default: {
      return state;
    }
  }
};

export { formReducer, initialFormState, FormActionType };
```

When the ChangeCountry action type is dispatched, we set the country value and reset the city value to it's default value, an empty string.

Now, let's make use of the formReducer that we just created. To do so, we'll create a new CheckoutForm component in a CheckoutForm.tsx file. In this new component, we'll add fields to collect a customer's billing details, specifically their country and city of residence.

```
import { useReducer } from 'react';
import { FormActionType, formReducer, initialFormState } from './formReducer';

const CheckoutForm = () => {
  const [state, dispatch] = useReducer(formReducer, initialFormState);

  return (
    <div>
      <div>
        <label>Country</label>
        <select
          name="country"
          value={state.country}
          onChange={(event) =>
            dispatch({
              type: FormActionType.ChangeCountry,
              payload: event.target.value,
            })
          }
        >
          <option value="">Select...</option>
          <option value="Canada">Canada</option>
          <option value="USA">USA</option>
        </select>
      </div>
      <div>
```

```
        <label>City</label>
        <input
          type="text"
          name="city"
          value={state.city}
          onChange={(event) =>
            dispatch({
              type: FormActionType.ChangeCity,
              payload: event.target.value,
            })
          }
        />
      </div>
      <div style={{ marginTop: '2rem' }}>
        <h5>Data in state</h5>
        {state.country && <p>Country: {state.country}</p>}
        {state.city && <p>City: {state.city}</p>}
      </div>
    </div>
  );
};

export { CheckoutForm };
```

When we modify either of the form fields, we'll see the data that is stored in state displayed below the form.

When we select a `country` and type in a `city` name, but then change the `country`, we'll notice that the `city` input gets cleared. This confirms that a change in `country` invalidates any `city` value that was previously stored in state.

The `useReducer` Hook was a better choice than the `useState` Hook for this example because we noticed dependencies that existed between the `country` and `city` state elements. The `city` state element relies on the changes to another state element, the `country` state element, in order to be updated properly.

useReducer and discriminate unions

We can make use of a TypeScript concept called *discriminate unions* to make `FormAction` more flexible so that it can support different `payload` types.

Let's do this by assigning a discriminate union type to `FormAction` in the `formReducer.ts` file. Let's also define a new `FormActionType` called `ChangeProducts` to introduce a different `payload` type.

```typescript
type FormState = {
  country: string;
  city: string;
  products: string[];
};

enum FormActionType {
  ChangeCountry = 'ChangeCountry',
  ChangeCity = 'ChangeCity',
  ChangeProducts = 'ChangeProducts',
}

type FormAction =
  | { type: FormActionType.ChangeCountry; payload: string }
  | { type: FormActionType.ChangeCity; payload: string }
  | { type: FormActionType.ChangeProducts; payload: string[] };

const initialFormState: FormState = {
  country: '',
  city: '',
  products: [],
};

const formReducer = (state: FormState, action: FormAction): FormState => {
  const { type, payload } = action;

  switch (type) {
    case FormActionType.ChangeCountry: {
      return {
        ...state,
        country: payload,
        city: '',
      };
    }
    case FormActionType.ChangeCity: {
      return {
        ...state,
        city: payload,
      };
    }
    case FormActionType.ChangeProducts: {
      return {
        ...state,
        products: payload,
      };
    }
    default: {
      return state;
    }
  }
```

```
};

export { formReducer, initialFormState, FormActionType };
```

FormAction is now a union of three object types. Each object has a common property called type. The type property in each object is a different FormActionType. This allows us to distinguish between action types. The payload for FormActionType.ChangeCountry and FormActionType.ChangeCity is a string, while the payload for FormActionType.ChangeProducts is an array of strings.

To support the new ChangeProducts action type, we added a products property to the FormState type. We defined products as an array of strings.

TypeScript creates automatic type guards for discriminate unions. If we write an if or a case statement to compare the type property of a FormAction object, the type of the payload received will need to match the one defined in the union type.

TypeScript will flag an error if we try to assign the payload of an action that is of type FormActionType.ChangeProducts to a variable that is not an array of strings.

```
const formReducer = (state: FormState, action: FormAction): FormState => {
  const { type, payload } = action;

  switch (type) {
    // ...
    case FormActionType.ChangeProducts: {
      // error
      const value: string = payload;

      // ...
    }
    // ...
    default: {
      return state;
    }
  }
};
```

The variable value will be underlined in red in VS Code due to the following error.

```
Type 'string[]' is not assignable to type 'string'.
```

Since the `type` of the `action` is specifically FormActionType.ChangeProducts, TypeScript knows that the corresponding `payload` of that action must be an array of strings. An array of strings cannot be assigned to the variable `value` because it only accepts strings.

Let's now use the new FormActionType.ChangeProducts action type that we just created. We'll implement it in the CheckoutForm component that we saw earlier. We can modify the form to dispatch the new action type.

To get started, we'll create an array of `products` that contains product objects with `name` and `price` properties. We'll iterate over the array of products and add a checkbox to the form for every product in the array. When we click on the checkbox beside a product to select or deselect it, the `products` state will be update.

```
import { ChangeEvent, useReducer } from 'react';
import { FormActionType, formReducer, initialFormState } from './formReducer';

const products = [
  {
    name: 'Product A',
    price: 9.99,
  },
  {
    name: 'Product B',
    price: 19.99,
  },
];

const CheckoutForm = () => {
  const [state, dispatch] = useReducer(formReducer, initialFormState);

  const isProductChecked = (name: string) => {
    return !!state.products.find((product) => product === name);
  }

  const onProductsChange = (event: ChangeEvent<HTMLInputElement>) => {
    let products;
    if (event.target.checked) {
      products = [...state.products, event.target.value];
    } else {
      products = state.products.filter(product => product !== event.target.value);
    }

    dispatch({
```

```
        type: FormActionType.ChangeProducts,
        payload: products,
      })
  }

  return (
    <div>
      <div>
        <label>Products</label>
        {products.map(({ name, price }) => {
          return (
            <li key={name}>
              <label htmlFor={name}>
                <input
                  id={name}
                  type="checkbox"
                  name={name}
                  value={name}
                  checked={isProductChecked(name)}
                  onChange={onProductsChange}
                />
                {name} ($ {price})
              </label>
            </li>
          );
        })}
      </div>
      <div>
        <label>Country</label>
        <select
          name="country"
          value={state.country}
          onChange={(event) =>
            dispatch({
              type: FormActionType.ChangeCountry,
              payload: event.target.value,
            })
          }
        >
          <option value="">Select...</option>
          <option value="Canada">Canada</option>
          <option value="USA">USA</option>
        </select>
      </div>
      <div>
        <label>City</label>
        <input
          type="text"
          name="city"
          value={state.city}
```

```
              onChange={(event) =>
                dispatch({
                  type: FormActionType.ChangeCity,
                  payload: event.target.value,
                })
              }
            />
        </div>
        <div>
          <h5>Data in state</h5>
          {state.products.length > 0 && <p>Products: {state.products.join(', ')
}</p>}
          {state.country && <p>Country: {state.country}</p>}
          {state.city && <p>City: {state.city}</p>}
        </div>
      </div>
    );
};

export { CheckoutForm };
```

We added an `isProductChecked` method to determine whether a checkbox should be displayed as checked or unchecked. This method checks whether the product name passed to it is present in the array of products stored in state.

We added an `onProductsChange` event handler function to dispatch an action using the new `FormActionType.ChangeProducts`. If a checkbox is checked, the action payload will consist of all product names already in state, plus the name of the newly selected product. If a checkbox is unchecked, the action payload will consist of all product names except the name of the newly deselected product. In both cases, the action payload will be assigned to the `products` property of the state object.

When we modify either of the form fields, we'll see the data that is stored in state displayed below the form.

useReducer recap

- For simple state management in React components, use the `useState` Hook.
- When managing complex state, using the `useReducer` Hook is a better choice than the `useState` Hook.
- It's possible to have multiple `useReducer` Hooks and multiple `useState` Hooks in the same component.
- Use the `useState` Hook to manage independent elements of state that have no relation to other state elements.
- Use the `useReducer` Hook to manage elements of state that need to be changed or updated together.
- Start with `useState` and only move to `useReducer` when you start noticing dependencies between state elements.

The useEffect Hook

The `useEffect` Hook has a reputation of being one of the hardest Hooks to grasp. We'll break it down step by step to make it easy to understand. It's named the `useEffect` Hook because it's used to perform side-effects in React functional components.

First, let's learn about what side-effects are and then we'll look at how to handle them with the `useEffect` Hook.

What are side-effects?

Side-effects are a functional programming concept. React functional components are meant to be *pure* functions. Given the same input props, a pure React functional component will always return the same output. Pure functions are predictable. If we know what their inputs are, we will always know what their output will be.

Side-effects, on the other hand, are not predictable. Side-effects are actions that require reaching outside of a React component. When we reach outside of a React component to perform a side-effect, we will not get a predictable result.

If we request blog posts from an API, we could get back an array of blog posts, we could get back an empty array, or we could get back an error message. The result is unpredictable.

The `useEffect` Hook gives us a way to perform side-effects within pure React functional components. The `useEffect` Hook is most commonly used to perform side-effects, such as:

- Requesting data from a server via an API.
- Using browser APIs (referencing the `document` or `window` objects).
- Using timer functions (`setTimeout` or `setInterval`).
- Subscribing to external data sources using WebSockets.
- Setting up event listeners using `addEventListener`.

How to use the useEffect Hook

To use the `useEffect` Hook, we must first import it. Then, we can use it in our component body. The `useEffect` Hook can receive two arguments, a callback function and an array of dependencies. The callback function is required, while the array of dependencies is not.

```
import { useEffect } from 'react';

const MyComponent = () => {
  useEffect(callbackFunction, dependencies);

  return <></>;
};

export { MyComponent };
```

The `callbackFunction` will perform the side-effect we want. That's where our side-effect logic goes. The `dependencies` argument is used to control when the `callbackFunction` should run. The `dependencies` argument is an optional array that can contain values that are used inside the `callbackFunction`.

The dependencies argument

The `useEffect` Hook allows us to perform side-effects at different times during the component lifecycle. There are 3 different ways that we can configure the `useEffect` callback function to run using the dependencies argument.

After every render

When the dependencies argument is not provided for the `useEffect` Hook, the callback function will run after every component render. It will run after the component first renders, and after every subsequent re-render of the component.

```
useEffect(() => {
  // Callback function runs after every render
});
```

After the first render

When the dependencies argument is an empty array, the callback function will run only after the first re-render of the component.

```
useEffect(() => {
  // Callback function runs after the first render
}, []);
```

When specific variables change

When the dependencies array contains values that are used inside the effect function, the callback function will run after the first re-render, and when any of the values in the dependencies array change.

React compares the current values of the dependencies with their previous values and re-runs the callback function if any of the values have changed.

```
useEffect(() => {
  // Runs after the first render
  // and when values for `variable1` or `variable2` change
}, [variable1, variable2]);
```

The most common ways that the dependencies argument is used with `useEffect` is either as an empty array, or as an array with dependency values. Rarely is it used with no dependencies argument at all. This would make it computationally expensive since it would run a side-effect on every component render.

Do we really need useEffect?

Can we not use `useEffect` and just put the code to handle side-effects within the component itself? Yes, but we should avoid doing so. If we perform a side-effect directly in the component body, it will get in the way of the rendering of the component and negatively impact that component's performance. Doing so could also produce unexpected results.

Let's look at a simple example to show how *not* to perform side-effects. In this example, we will try setting the document title using a component prop.

```
import { useEffect } from "react";

type Props = {
  name: string;
};

const User = ({ name }: Props) => {
  document.title = name;
  // Avoid side-effects in the component body

  return <h1>{name}</h1>;
};

export { User };
```

While this does still work - setting the document title to whatever name is passed in to the User component - it should be avoided. In the example above, the document title will be set every time time that the User component renders. This can lead to performance issues.

If side-effects need to be performed, they should be separated from the rendering process of a component. Side-effects should be performed after the component finishes rendering.

This is exactly what the useEffect Hook allows us to do. With the useEffect Hook, we can reach outside of the component and perform a side-effect, without affecting the component's rendering performance.

Let's re-write the example above using the useEffect Hook.

```
import { useEffect } from "react";

type Props = {
  name: string;
};

const User = ({ name }: Props) => {
  useEffect(() => {
    document.title = name;
  }, [name]);

  return <h1>{name}</h1>;
};

export { User };
```

Setting the document title is a side-effect because it reaches outside of the component and interfaces with the browser API to access the document object. Since it's a side-effect, we should use useEffect for it.

We don't want the setting of the document title to happen every time the User component renders. We only want the document title to be set when the component first renders and when the component's name prop changes. Therefore, we provided a dependencies array and added name to it.

Fetching data with useEffect

A common reason to use the useEffect Hook is to fetch data from an API. The following example will fetch facts about cats from a cat fact API when the component first renders.

```
import { useEffect, useState } from 'react';

const API_URL = 'https://catfact.ninja/facts';

type Fact = {
  fact: string;
};

const CatFacts = () => {
  const [facts, setFacts] = useState<Fact[]>([]);

  useEffect(() => {
    async function fetchFacts() {
      const response = await fetch(API_URL);
      const { data } = await response.json();
      setFacts(data);
    }

    fetchFacts();
  }, []);

  return (
    <ul>
      {facts.map(({ fact }) => (
        <li>{fact}</li>
      ))}
    </ul>
  );
};

export { CatFacts };
```

When the component first renders, the `useEffect` Hook initiates a fetch request by calling its inner `fetchFacts` function.

When the async fetch request completes, the `setFacts` state setter function updates the `facts` state with the cat facts that were returned by the API.

To make async requests with `useEffect`, the `async` function must be placed within the `useEffect` callback function. By placing the `async` function at the top of the callback function, we can easily trigger it right after defining it.

The `useEffect` callback function cannot itself be an `async` function. This means that we cannot define the `async` function outside of the `useEffect` callback, add it as a dependency to the dependencies array, and then `await` it within the callback. This won't work.

The dependency pitfall

A common pitfall that developers experience when using the `useEffect` Hook is the dependency pitfall. It causes an infinite loop of component renders.

This pitfall often occurs when updating component state within the `useEffect` Hook, but without having that state variable set as a dependency in the dependencies array.

Let's take a look at an example that will purposely trigger this pitfall. The component for this example will provide a text input to collect user input. It will then show the user the number of changes that have made to the text input.

```
import { ChangeEvent, useEffect, useState } from 'react';

const User = () => {
  const [value, setValue] = useState('');
  const [count, setCount] = useState(-1);

  useEffect(() => {
    setCount(count + 1);
  });
  // Bad: no dependencies array

  const onChange = (event: React.ChangeEvent<HTMLInputElement>) => setValue(event.target.value);

  return (
    <div>
      <input type="text" value={value} onChange={onChange} />
      <p>Changes: {count}</p>
    </div>
  );
};

export { User };
```

In this example, `useEffect` is used without any dependencies array. This means that it will run after every component render. This causes the `count` state variable to increment by 1 uncontrollably, up to infinity. This happens right when the component first loads, even if we haven't changed any text in the input yet.

An infinite loop has been created. After the component's initial render, the `useEffect` Hook runs its callback function, which updates the state via `setCount`. This state update triggers a component re-render. When the component re-renders, the `useEffect` Hook once again runs its

138

callback function that updates the state again. This cycle forms the infinite loop. It continues for as long as we keep the component loaded in our web browser.

We can fix this infinite loop by providing a dependency to the useEffect dependencies array. We want the value for count to increment only when the value of the text input changes. Therefore, we just need to add the value state variable as a dependency to useEffect.

```
import { ChangeEvent, useEffect, useState } from 'react';

const User = () => {
  const [value, setValue] = useState('');
  const [count, setCount] = useState(-1);

  useEffect(() => {
    setCount(count + 1);
  }, [value]);
  // Good: `count` increments only when `value` changes

  const onChange = (event: ChangeEvent<HTMLInputElement>) => setValue(event.target.value);

  return (
    <div>
      <input type="text" value={value} onChange={onChange} />
      <p>Changes: {count}</p>
    </div>
  );
};

export { User };
```

This change fixes the infinite loop. Now, when we type into the text input, the value for count reflects the exact number of changes made to the text input.

The object pitfall

Another common pitfall that developers experience when using the useEffect Hook is the object pitfall. We must be careful when using objects in the dependencies array. Similar to the dependency pitfall above, this pitfall also creates an infinite loop.

Objects, arrays, and functions are more difficult to use as useEffect dependencies, compared to primitives like strings, numbers, or booleans. The reason for this is because React performs referential equality checks on objects, arrays, and functions in the useEffect dependencies array.

When it comes to referential equality, React checks to see if the object of the current render points to the same object in memory of the previous render.

Referential equality of two objects means that they point to the exact same reference in memory. This is different from structural equality, which means that two objects have the same value.

The `useEffect` Hook will only skip re-running its callback function when objects in the dependencies array are the exact same objects, pointing to the same memory reference. If a new object is created during a component re-render, that new object gets a new memory reference, breaking referential equality, thereby causing `useEffect` to re-run its callback function.

Consider the following example of a `User` component that counts the number of changes made to a user's name.

```
import { ChangeEvent, useEffect, useState } from "react";

const User = () => {
  const [user, setUser] = useState({ name: "", changes: -1 });

  useEffect(() => {
    setUser({ ...user, changes: user.changes + 1 });
  }, [user]);
  // Danger: user is an object

  const onChange = (event: ChangeEvent<HTMLInputElement>) => {
    setUser({ ...user, name: event.target.value });
  };

  return (
    <div>
      <p>Name: <input type="text" value={user.name} onChange={onChange} /></p>
      <p>Changes: {user.changes}</p>
    </div>
  );
};

export { User };
```

Within the `useEffect` callback function, a new object is created within the `setUser` state setter function call. Though the dependencies array is defined for `useEffect`, it contains the `user` object. Let's see how this affects execution.

During the first render of the User component above, the useEffect Hook runs its callback function, creating a new user object with its changes property set to 0. The User component will then re-render, triggered by the setUser state setter function call.

During the re-render, the useEffect Hook will detect that the user object in its dependencies array has changed and is now a new object. As a result, it will re-run its callback function, creating an infinite loop that increments the user object's changes property an infinite number of times.

Since a new user object is created with every render, the useEffect referential equality check will fail, causing useEffect to run its callback function on every render.

The simplest way to fix the infinite loop, created by the circular creation of new objects, is to avoid using references to objects in the useEffect dependencies array. Instead of having useEffect depend on the whole user object, it should only depend on the specific object properties that are used within the useEffect callback function.

Let's fix the previous example by updating the dependencies array to contain user.name instead of just user.

```
import { ChangeEvent, useEffect, useState } from "react";

const User = () => {
  const [user, setUser] = useState({ name: "", changes: -1 });

  useEffect(() => {
    setUser({ ...user, changes: user.changes + 1 });
  }, [user.name]);
  // Good: no object reference

  const onChange = (event: React.ChangeEvent<HTMLInputElement>) => {
    setUser({ ...user, name: event.target.value });
  };

  return (
    <div>
      <p>
        Name:
        <input type="text" value={user.name} onChange={onChange} />
      </p>
      <p>Changes: {user.changes}</p>
    </div>
  );
}
```

```
export { User }
```

The useEffect callback function uses only the name property of the user object, so we should only be adding the name property to the dependencies array.

Since the name property of the user object is a string, the useEffect callback function will now only run when the value of user's name changes. Other properties within the user object can change, but the useEffect callback function will not re-run unless the name property's value changes.

The props-in-state pitfall

A common pitfall is putting the component's props as-is into state by using the useEffect Hook. This is usually done because the developer doesn't realize that a component automatically re-renders when its props change. There is no need to manually manage component prop changes.

This common mistake causes an unnecessary re-render. One re-render happens when the prop changes, and another re-render happens when the state is changed by the state setter function that is called within the useEffect Hook.

Let's take a look at an example of the props-in-state pitfall.

```
import { useEffect, useState } from "react";

type Props = {
  value: number;
}

const ValueDisplay = ({ value }: Props) => {
  const [countValue, setCountValue] = useState<number>(0);

  // runs when the 'value' prop changes
  useEffect(() => {
    // saves the latest value to state
    setCountValue(value);
  }, [value]);

  // for logging purposes (runs on every render)
  useEffect(() => {
    console.log(`Rendered with value ${value}`);
  });

  return <p>{countValue}</p>;
};
```

```
const ValueChanger = () => {
  const [value, setValue] = useState<number>(0);

  return (
    <div>
      <ValueDisplay value={value} />
      <button onClick={() => setValue(Math.random())}>Change Value</button>
    </div>
  );
};

export { ValueChanger };
```

Two lines are logged to the console for every "Change Value" button click from the ValueChanger component. This happens because the ValueDisplay component will re-render twice.

The first re-render happens every time the value prop for the ValueDisplay component changes. This occurs whenever the "Change Value" button is clicked. The second re-render happens because there is a useEffect in the ValueDisplay component that calls the setCountValue state setter function.

We actually do not need any state in the ValueDisplay component. We can display its value prop directly. Since components automatically re-render when their props change, the ValueDisplay component will always be in sync with the latest values passed in to it via its props.

We can simplify the above example by remove the unnecessary useEffect Hook in the ValueDisplay component.

```
import { useState } from "react";

type Props = {
  value: number;
}

const ValueDisplay = ({ value }: Props) => {
  // for logging purposes (runs on every render)
  useEffect(() => {
    console.log(`Rendered with value ${value}`);
  });

  return (
    <p>{value}</p>
  );
```

```
};

const ValueChanger = () => {
  const [value, setValue] = useState<number>(0);

  return (
    <div>
      <ValueDisplay value={value} />
      <button onClick={() => setValue(Math.random())}>Change Value</button>
    </div>
  );
};

export { ValueChanger };
```

With these changes, the `ValueDisplay` component will only re-render once for every change to its props. Now, every time the "Change Value" button is clicked in the `ValueChanger` component, only one line is logged to the console by the `ValueDisplay` component.

Side-effect cleanup

Side-effect cleanup is the process of cleaning up any side-effects that were created by a component within the `useEffect` Hook.

Examples of common side-effect cleanup tasks are:

- Closing a web socket.
- Clearing a timer.
- Cancelling a subscription.
- Cancelling a fetch request.
- Removing an event listener.

Both asynchronous and synchronous side-effects need to be cleaned up. If the side-effect is asynchronous, such as making an API call, then we must cancel the request when the component unmounts. This will clean up any resources associated with the request. If the side-effect is synchronous, such as setting up an event listener, it's still important to clean up the event listener to prevent memory leaks.

When the callback function for the `useEffect` Hook returns a function, React will perform a side-effect cleanup. Performing side-effect cleanups helps optimize the performance of components.

Side-effect cleanups are done when a component re-renders, just before the next scheduled side-effect runs, and when a component unmounts.

Let's take a look at how to use a cleanup function within `useEffect`.

```
const MyComponent = () => {
  useEffect(() => {
    // Side-effect logic...

    return () => {
      // Side-effect cleanup
    };
  }, []);

  return (
    // ...
  );
}
```

Let's look at some examples where the side-effect cleanup is important.

Cleaning up timer functions

Let's take a look at a `TimerLogger` component that logs a message to the console every two seconds.

```
import { useState, useEffect } from 'react';

type Props = {
  message: string;
}

const TimerLogger = ({ message }: Props) => {
  useEffect(() => {
    setInterval(() => {
      console.log(message);
    }, 2000);
  }, [message]);

  return <p>Logging "{message}" to the console</p>;
}

const Message = () => {
  const [message, setMessage] = useState("Hello World");

  return (
    <div>
      <h1>Type a message</h1>
```

```
      <input
        type="text"
        value={message}
        onChange={(e) => setMessage(e.target.value)}
      />
      <TimerLogger message={message} />
    </div>
  );
}

export { Message };
```

If we run this example and change the "Hello World" message to something else, such as "Hello Worlds", both messages will be logged to the console every 2 seconds. However, only the latest message should be logged to the console.

The reason for this is because we didn't clean up the side-effect produced by `setInterval`. We must cancel the previous timer before starting a new timer.

Let's modify the `TimerLogger` component from the example above so that it returns a cleanup function within `useEffect`. This cleanup function will stop the previous timer before starting a new timer by using `clearInterval`.

```
const TimerLogger = ({ message }: Props) => {
  useEffect(() => {
    const id = setInterval(() => {
      console.log(message);
    }, 2000);

    return () => {
      clearInterval(id);
    };
  }, [message]);

  return <p>Logging "{message}" to the console</p>;
}
```

With the cleanup function in place, only the last message entered into the text input will be logged to the console. This is because all previously running timers get cleaned up by the cleanup function.

When the value of `message` in the dependencies array of the `useEffect` Hook changes, the cleanup function will run first Then, the `useEffect` callback function will run again with the new value for `message`.

Cleaning up event listeners

The `useEffect` Hook helps us to add and remove event listeners from our component. The following example will add and remove event listeners for a `keyup` event, which occurs when a user releases a key on their keyboard.

```
import { useEffect } from "react";

const ListenerLogger = () => {
  useEffect(() => {
    const handleKeyUp = (e: KeyboardEvent) => {
      console.log('Key up: ', e.key);
    };

    window.addEventListener('keyup', handleKeyUp);

    return () => window.removeEventListener('keyup', handleKeyUp);
  }, []);

  return <div>Logging "keyup" events to the console</div>;
};

export { ListenerLogger };
```

An empty dependencies array is used for the `useEffect` Hook so that it only runs when the component first mounts. This is because we only want to add the event listener once, when the component first mounts.

Within the `useEffect` Hook, a `keyup` event listener is added via the `addEventListener` method. The `useEffect` Hook returns a function for side-effect cleanup purposes. In this case, we want to clean up the event listener. The cleanup function will remove the event listener for `keyup` when the component unmounts by using the `removeEventListener` method.

The first parameter of the `addEventListener` and `removeEventListener` functions is the type of the event. The second parameter is a function that is invoked when an event of the specified type occurs.

Cleaning up event listeners is important because it helps prevent memory leaks in React applications.

Cleaning up fetch requests

When making fetch requests from a React component, we must look out for race conditions. A race condition is when two different requests "race" against each other and arrive in a different order than we might expected.

Let's say we have a component that accepts a prop. The component then uses that prop to fetch data within `useEffect` and displays the result. We may notice a strange behavior coming from this component, where it sometimes displays accurate data and sometimes displays stale data.

This strange behavior is a race condition. If the component's prop used to fetch data changes fast enough, multiple requests for data will be made in a short time. The component will display different results depending on which request completes first. There is no guarantee that all requests will complete in the order that they were received.

To fix the race condition, we need to add a cleanup function to `useEffect` so that it will ignore stale responses. All responses except the last requested one will be ignored.

In the following example, we will fetch Star Wars characters from a `Character` component. We'll fetch a character when the component first loads, and also when the "Fetch Character" button is clicked.

We will add a random wait period of up to 10 seconds between fetch requests using `setTimeout`. This will make the race conditions more obvious when we run the example.

If we click on the "Fetch Character" button quickly multiple times, we'll notice that most of the time, the fetch requests will finish out of order. The slowest request to complete will be displayed last, but it won't always be the last request that was actually made.

```
import { useState, useEffect } from "react";

const API_URL = 'https://swapi.dev/api/people';

type StarWarsCharacter = {
  name: string;
};

type Props = {
  id: number;
};
```

```
const Character = ({ id }: Props) => {
  const [data, setData] = useState<StarWarsCharacter | null>(null);
  const [fetchedId, setFetchedId] = useState<number | null>(null);

  useEffect(() => {
    const fetchData = async () => {
      setTimeout(async () => {
        const response = await fetch(`${API_URL}/${id}`);
        const newData = await response.json();
        setFetchedId(id);
        setData(newData);
      }, Math.round(Math.random() * 10000));
    };

    fetchData();
  }, [id]);

  if (!data) {
    return null;
  }

  return (
    <div>
      <p style={{ color: fetchedId === id ? 'green' : 'red' }}>
        Data for ID {fetchedId}
      </p>
      <p>{data.name}</p>
    </div>
  );
};

const Characters = () => {
  const [characterId, setCharacterId] = useState<number>(1);

  const handleClick = () => {
    // Pick a random character id (max of 82 characters)
    const id = Math.floor(Math.random() * 82) + 1;
    setCharacterId(id);
  };

  return (
    <div>
      <p>Fetching character with ID {characterId}</p>
      <button type="button" onClick={handleClick}>
        Fetch Character
      </button>
      <hr />
      <Character id={characterId} />
    </div>
  );
```

```
};

export { Characters };
```

In one sequence, I clicked the "Fetch Character" button three times. The `Characters` component displayed "Fetching character with ID 18". However, I saw "Data for ID 5" displayed by the `Character` component. What happened was that the last fetch request with an `id` of 18 finished sooner than the second-last fetch request with an `id` of 5. We've caught a race condition.

We can fix the race condition by using the `useEffect` side-effect cleanup function. There are two different approaches that we can take to achieve this.

- Use the Web Browser API's `AbortController`.
- Use a boolean flag.

Let's take a look at both approaches.

Fix the race condition with an AbortController

The `AbortController` is part of the Web Browser API and it allows us to abort requests. To use it, we must pass the AbortController's `signal` to the fetch request so that we can abort it when needed. We then abort the fetch request in the `useEffect` side-effect cleanup function.

Let's fix the Star Wars characters example by defining a cleanup function for `useEffect`. The cleanup function will make use of the `AbortController`.

```
import { useState, useEffect } from "react";

const API_URL = 'https://swapi.dev/api/people';

type StarWarsCharacter = {
  name: string;
};

type Props = {
  id: number;
};

const Character = ({ id }: Props) => {
  const [data, setData] = useState<StarWarsCharacter | null>(null);
  const [fetchedId, setFetchedId] = useState<number | null>(null);

  useEffect(() => {
    const abortController = new AbortController();
```

```
    const fetchData = async () => {
      setTimeout(async () => {
        const response = await fetch(`${API_URL}/${id}`, {
          signal: abortController.signal,
        });
        const newData = await response.json();
        setFetchedId(id);
        setData(newData);
      }, Math.round(Math.random() * 10000));
    };

    fetchData();

    return () => {
      abortController.abort();
    };
  }, [id]);

  if (!data) {
    return null;
  }

  return (
    <div>
      <p style={{ color: fetchedId === id ? 'green' : 'red' }}>
        Data for ID {fetchedId}
      </p>
      <p>{data.name}</p>
    </div>
  );
};

const Characters = () => {
  const [characterId, setCharacterId] = useState<number>(1);

  const handleClick = () => {
    // Pick a random character id (max of 82 characters)
    const id = Math.floor(Math.random() * 82) + 1;
    setCharacterId(id);
  };

  return (
    <div>
      <p>Fetching character with ID {characterId}</p>
      <button type="button" onClick={handleClick}>
        Fetch Character
      </button>
      <hr />
      <Character id={characterId} />
```

```
    </div>
  );
};

export { Characters };
```

When the `Character` component is in the middle of performing a fetch request, but it receives a new value for the `id` prop, that fetch request will be aborted. A new fetch request using the new `id` value will be performed.

Here's what we did in this solution:

- Initialized an `AbortController` in the `useEffect` callback function.
- Passed the `signal` returned from the `AbortController` to our fetch request.
- Called the `abort` function inside the `useEffect` side-effect cleanup function.

Now, when we click on the "Fetch Character" button quickly multiple times, the last fetch request to be completed and displayed always corresponds to the last character `id` that was generated.

Fix the race condition with a boolean flag

Similar to the `AbortController`, a boolean flag can act as a switch that blocks stale requests.

Let's define a boolean variable called `active` with a value of `true`. We will define it at the start of the `useEffect` in the `Character` component. In the side-effect cleanup function, we will set `active` to `false`.

```
import { useState, useEffect } from "react";

const API_URL = 'https://swapi.dev/api/people';

type StarWarsCharacter = {
  name: string;
};

type Props = {
  id: number;
};

const Character = ({ id }: Props) => {
  const [data, setData] = useState<StarWarsCharacter | null>(null);
  const [fetchedId, setFetchedId] = useState<number | null>(null);

  useEffect(() => {
    let active = true;
```

```
    const fetchData = async () => {
      setTimeout(async () => {
        const response = await fetch(`${API_URL}/${id}`);
        const newData = await response.json();
        if (active) {
          setFetchedId(id);
          setData(newData);
        }
      }, Math.round(Math.random() * 10000));
    };

    fetchData();

    return () => {
      active = false;
    };
  }, [id]);

  if (!data) {
    return null;
  }

  return (
    <div>
      <p style={{ color: fetchedId === id ? 'green' : 'red' }}>
        Data for ID {fetchedId}
      </p>
      <p>{data.name}</p>
    </div>
  );
};

const Characters = () => {
  const [characterId, setCharacterId] = useState<number>(1);

  const handleClick = () => {
    // Pick a random character id (max of 82 characters)
    const id = Math.floor(Math.random() * 82) + 1;
    setCharacterId(id);
  };

  return (
    <div>
      <p>Fetching character with ID {characterId}</p>
      <button type="button" onClick={handleClick}>
        Fetch Character
      </button>
      <hr />
      <Character id={characterId} />
```

```
      </div>
    );
};

export { Characters };
```

Every time the `id` prop for the `Character` component changes, the component re-renders. Every re-render causes the `useEffect` cleanup function to run, which sets the `active` boolean flag to `false`. When `active` is set to `false`, any stale requests will not be permitted to update the state for `data` and `fetchedId`. Stale requests are blocked from interfering with the accurate display of character data.

Race conditions, caused by multiple simultaneous fetch requests, will still occur with both of the solutions that we've seen. However, only the result from the last fetch request will be considered and displayed by the `Character` component.

When not to use the useEffect Hook

Overusing the `useEffect` Hook, when it's not really needed, is one of the most common React mistakes. By avoiding unnecessary usage of `useEffect`, we can make our code less susceptible to bugs, easier to trace, and more performant.

The `useEffect` Hook causes us to step outside of React so that we can synchronize our React components with an external system, such as the browser DOM, or an API, via network requests. If we don't have to synchronize our components with an external system, we should not be using the `useEffect` Hook.

There's two cases in React where effects are often used, but they are actually not necessary. The two cases are:

- **Transforming data for rendering**: We can apply transformations to props or state within our component and then assign those transformations to new variables. We don't need `useEffect` for this. Our transformation code will automatically re-run whenever the props or state changes. Data in React flows from the top-down. If we transform data within top-level components, that transformed data can flow downward to child components via props.
- **Handling user events**: We don't need `useEffect` to handle user events. It's better to handle user events in event handlers. In the event handler functions, we know exactly what event occurred. If it was a button click event, we know exactly which button was clicked. However,

when an effect runs, we don't know which events occurred from within the useEffect Hook. If multiple buttons were clicked, we can't tell which button was clicked.

We can avoid unnecessary component re-renders by avoiding effects for the cases mentioned above.

Let's take a look at a few examples where useEffect is not really necessary. We will refactor these examples to remove useEffect, simplifying the code and making it more performant.

Updating state based on other state

Suppose there's a UserForm component with two state variables, firstName and lastName. We want to calculate a fullName from these two state variables by concatenating them. We want fullName to update whenever firstName or lastName change.

One inefficient solution is to add a fullName state variable and to update fullName in an effect.

```
import { useState, useEffect } from "react";

const UserForm = () => {
  const [firstName, setFirstName] = useState<string>('John');
  const [lastName, setLastName] = useState<string>('Smith');
  // Bad: redundant state causes a useless Effect
  const [fullName, setFullName] = useState<string>('');

  // Bad: useless Effect
  useEffect(() => {
    setFullName(`${firstName} ${lastName}`);
  }, [firstName, lastName]);

  return (
    <>
      <input type="text" name="firstName" value={firstName} onChange={(event) => setFirstName(event?.target.value)} />
      <input type="text" name="lastName" value={lastName} onChange={(event) => setLastName(event?.target.value)} />
      <p>Full name: {fullName}</p>
    </>
  );
};

export { UserForm };
```

The `fullName` state is redundant because we can compute it from what is already stored in state, via `firstName` and `lastName`. Introducing this redundant state variable, `fullName`, means that we need to add a `useEffect` Hook to keep it synchronized whenever `firstName` or `lastName` change.

We actually don't need an effect for computing the `fullName`. We can simply use an local variable to compute the full name of the user. Whenever the `UserForm` component re-renders, the full name will be automatically re-computed.

```
import { useState } from "react";

const UserForm = () => {
  const [firstName, setFirstName] = useState<string>('John');
  const [lastName, setLastName] = useState<string>('Smith');
  // Good: compute it during rendering
  const fullName = `${firstName} ${lastName}`;

  return (
    <>
      <input type="text" name="firstName" value={firstName} onChange={(event) => setFirstName(event?.target.value)} />
      <input type="text" name="lastName" value={lastName} onChange={(event) => setLastName(event?.target.value)} />
      <p>Full name: {fullName}</p>
    </>
  );
};

export { UserForm };
```

The result is the same, but this solution requires less code and is more efficient.

Resetting state when a prop changes

Let's take a look at a `BlogPost` component that renders blog posts to the screen. It receives a `postId` prop. This component also has a text input for a comment, which gets stored in state.

After testing out this component, we notice a problem. We notice that navigating to different blog posts does not reset the `comment` state. This can cause the wrong comment to be posted on the wrong blog post. In order to fix this issue, we need to clear the `comment` state whenever the `postId` prop changes.

Let's take a look at the inefficient solution below that uses an effect.

```
import { useState, useEffect } from "react";

type Props = {
  postId: number;
}

const BlogPost = ({ postId }: Props) => {
  const [comment, setComment] = useState('');

  // Bad: effect used to reset state when prop changes
  useEffect(() => {
    setComment('');
  }, [postId]);

  return (
    <>
      <p>Post ID: {postId}</p>
      <p>Comment: <input type="text" name="comment" value={comment} onChange={(event) => setComment(event.target.value)} /></p>
    </>
  );
};

export { BlogPost };
```

The useEffect Hook is used to reset the comment state whenever the postId prop changes. However, useEffect isn't needed here.

To simulate changes to the postId prop on the BlogPost component, let's set up an interval counter that increments the postId every four seconds. We can do this in the same file as the BlogPost component.

```
const BlogPostApp = () => {
  const [id, setId] = useState(1);

  useEffect(() => {
    const interval = setInterval(() => {
      setId(id => id + 1);
    }, 4000);

    return () => clearInterval(interval);
  }, []);

  return <BlogPost postId={id} />
};

export { BlogPostApp };
```

If we input some text in the comment input, we'll notice that the comment gets cleared every 4 seconds, when the `postId` changes. This confirms that the solution works, but it is inefficient.

It's an inefficient solution because the `BlogPost` component will render first with a stale state value for `comment`, and then it will re-render due to the invocation of `setComment('')` within the `useEffect` callback function.

A better solution is to inform React that each blog post is different from the other blog posts. We can do this by using an explicit `key` for each blog post.

Let's split the `BlogPost` component into an outer `BlogPost` component and an inner `Post` component. Then, we'll pass a `key` attribute from the outer component to the inner component.

```
import { useState, useEffect } from "react";

type Props = {
  postId: number;
}

const Post = ({ postId }: Props) => {
  // Good: state automatically reset on key change from BlogPost
  const [comment, setComment] = useState('');

  return (
    <>
      <p>Post ID: {postId}</p>
      <p>Comment: <input type="text" name="comment" value={comment} onChange={(event) => setComment(event.target.value)} /></p>
    </>
  );
};

const BlogPost = ({ postId }: Props) => {
  return (
    <Post
      postId={postId}
      key={postId}
    />
  );
};

export { BlogPost };
```

By passing `postId` as a key to the inner `Post` component, we're telling React to treat each `Post` component with a different `postId` key as a unique component. Each blog post should not share any state with other blog posts that have a different `postId`.

Whenever the `postId` key changes, React will reset the state of the `Post` component and all of its children. As a result, the `comment` state and the comment text input will be automatically cleared when transitioning between blog posts.

It's important to recognize that the `key` on the `Post` component is not a prop. We cannot retrieve `key` from the `Post` component as we do with props. It's simply a unique identifier.

The outer `BlogPost` component should be the only one exported and made visible to other files in our React project. The inner `Post` component only needs to be known by `BlogPost`. Other components that need to use the `BlogPost` component will not need to pass a key to it. Those components will only need to pass a `postId` prop. `BlogPost` will handle the responsibility of passing `postId` as a key to the inner `Post` component.

This solution makes us of *information-hiding*, whereby the implementation of the `key` attribute is kept internal to the `BlogPost` component, and is hidden from other components that use `BlogPost`.

Adjusting state when a prop changes

Let's consider the case where we need to modify a part of state when a prop changes. Let's say that we have a `List` component that receives a list of `items` as a prop. This `List` component then keeps track of the selected list item using a state variable. What we'll need to do is to reset the selected list item whenever the list of items in the `items` prop changes.

Let's start by taking a look at the inefficient solution. It uses an effect that resets the state for the selected item every time that the `items` prop changes.

We'll simulate changes to the `items` prop by using an interval timer to alternate between two lists every 4 seconds.

```
import { useState, useEffect } from "react";
type Item = { id: number; name: string };
type Props = { items: Item[] };
```

```
const List = ({ items }: Props) => {
  const [selection, setSelection] = useState<Item | null>(null);

  // Bad: using an effect to update state when prop changes
  useEffect(() => {
    setSelection(null);
  }, [items]);

  return (
    <div>
      <ul>
        {items.map((item) => (
          <li key={item.id} onClick={() => setSelection(item)}>
            {item.name}
          </li>
        ))}
      </ul>
      <p>Selection: {selection?.name ?? 'None'}</p>
    </div>
  );
};

const CharacterList = () => {
  const items1 = [{ id: 1, name: "Mario" }, { id: 2, name: "Luigi" }];
  const items2 = [{ id: 3, name: "Toad" }, { id: 4, name: "Peach" }];

  const [id, setId] = useState(1);

  useEffect(() => {
    const interval = setInterval(() => {
      setId(id => id === 1 ? 2 : 1);
    }, 4000);

    return () => clearInterval(interval);
  }, []);

  return (
    <List items={id === 1 ? items1 : items2} />
  );
};

export { CharacterList };
```

When the `items` prop changes, the `List` component will render with a stale state value for the selected item, `selection`. The value will be stale until React runs the `List` component's effects.

Another issue with this solution is that resetting the state for `selection` within `useEffect` triggers a component re-render for the `List` component and any of its child components.

We can avoid resetting state completely by computing the selected item and storing it in a local variable. Instead of storing the entire selected item, which is redundant, we can simply store the selected item's id.

```
import { useState, useEffect } from "react";

type Item = { id: number; name: string };

type Props = { items: Item[] };

const List = ({ items }: Props) => {
  const [selectedId, setSelectedId] = useState<number | null>(null);
  // Good: compute selected item during renders
  const selection = items.find(({ id }) => id === selectedId) ?? null;

  return (
    <div>
      <ul>
        {items.map((item) => (
          <li key={item.id} onClick={() => setSelectedId(item.id)}>
            {item.name}
          </li>
        ))}
      </ul>
      <p>Selection: {selection?.name ?? 'None'}</p>
    </div>
  );
};

const CharacterList = () => {
  const items1 = [{ id: 1, name: "Mario" }, { id: 2, name: "Luigi" }];
  const items2 = [{ id: 3, name: "Toad" }, { id: 4, name: "Peach" }];

  const [id, setId] = useState(1);

  useEffect(() => {
    const interval = setInterval(() => {
      setId(id => id === 1 ? 2 : 1);
    }, 4000);

    return () => clearInterval(interval);
  }, []);

  return (
    <List items={id === 1 ? items1 : items2} />
  );
};
```

```
export { CharacterList };
```

If the list item clicked on by the user is in the list, it will be the selected item. If the list item clicked on by the user is no longer in the list, possibly because the `items` prop has changed, then the selected item computed during rendering will be `null`. No matching item will be found.

Modifying state based on props, or other state, makes the flow of data very hard to understand, test, and debug. It is best to avoid it. Instead, we should reset state with a key (as we saw above), or use local variables to store computed values during component renders (as we just saw).

Making an event-related POST request

Let's consider a user profile form in a `ProfilePage` component. It needs to send two POST requests to an API. The first POST request must send analytics information when the form component mounts. The second POST request must save the user's profile details when the form is submitted.

For the sake of simplicity, we'll use `console.log` statements in the `ProfilePage` component as placeholders for where the actual POST requests would go.

```
import { useState, useEffect, FormEvent } from "react";

type ProfileData = {
  firstName: string;
  lastName: string;
};

const ProfilePage = () => {
  const [firstName, setFirstName] = useState('');
  const [lastName, setLastName] = useState('');
  const [profileData, setProfileData] = useState<ProfileData | null>(null);

  // Good: analytics event sent when the form mounts
  useEffect(() => {
    console.log('POST request - ProfilePageView analytics event');
  }, []);

  // Bad: POST request is event-related. Effect not needed
  useEffect(() => {
    if (profileData !== null) {
      console.log('POST request - saving user profile');
    }
  }, [profileData]);

  const handleSubmit = (e: FormEvent<HTMLFormElement>) => {
```

162

```
    e.preventDefault();
    setProfileData({ firstName, lastName });
  };

  return (
    <div>
      <form onSubmit={handleSubmit}>
        <input
          type="text"
          name="firstName"
          placeholder="First name"
          value={firstName}
          onChange={(e) => setFirstName(e.target.value)} />
        <input
          type="text"
          name="lastName"
          placeholder="Last name"
          value={lastName}
          onChange={(e) => setLastName(e.target.value)} />
        <button type="submit">Submit</button>
      </form>
    </div>
  );
};

export { ProfilePage };
```

The analytics POST request is fine in the useEffect Hook. An empty dependencies array will ensure that this effect only runs when the component mounts. This POST request is a good case for the useEffect Hook because we want to capture an analytics event only when the component is first mounted.

The POST request to save the user profile is within a useEffect Hook. While this works, it is an inefficient solution. We only need to send this POST request when a user submits the form. the useEffect Hook is not needed for this POST request because we can simply handle it in an event handler.

Since the POST request to save the user profile is tied to a user event, we can move it into the handleSubmit event handler function. This will allow us to get rid of the unnecessary useEffect Hook, as well as the unnecessary profileData state.

```
import { useState, useEffect } from "react";

const ProfilePage = () => {
  const [firstName, setFirstName] = useState('');
```

```
  const [lastName, setLastName] = useState('');

  // Good: analytics event sent when the form mounts
  useEffect(() => {
    console.log('POST request - ProfilePageView analytics event');
  }, []);

  const handleSubmit = (e) => {
    e.preventDefault();
    // Good: event-related POST request is in an event handler
    console.log('POST request - saving user profile');
  };

  return (
    <div>
      <form onSubmit={handleSubmit}>
        <input
          type="text"
          name="firstName"
          value={firstName}
          onChange={(e) => setFirstName(e.target.value)} />
        <input
          type="text"
          name="lastName"
          value={lastName}
          onChange={(e) => setLastName(e.target.value)} />
        <button type="submit">Submit</button>
      </form>
    </div>
  );
};

export { ProfilePage };
```

Any side-effects caused by a user interaction belong in an event handler function. We saw this type of side-effect with the saving of the user profile when the form is submitted.

Side-effects caused by a component lifecycle event belong in the useEffect Hook. We saw this type of side-effect with the tracking of an analytics event every time the component mounts.

Passing fetched data to the parent

Let's consider a scenario where we need a parent component to know about the data that is fetched by a particular child component. The parent component is a MyProfile component and the child component is a MyActivity component.

An inefficient solution would be to have the child component fetch the data and then pass it to the parent component via the useEffect Hook. Let's take a look at this solution below.

```
import { useState, useEffect } from "react";

const API_URL = 'https://www.boredapi.com/api/activity';

type Activity = {
  activity: string;
  type: string;
}

type Props = {
  onFetched: (data: Activity | null) => void;
}

const MyActivity = ({ onFetched }: Props) => {
  const [data, setData] = useState<Activity | null>(null);

  // Bad: Passing data to the parent via `onFetched` in an effect
  useEffect(() => {
    async function fetchActivity() {
      const response = await fetch(API_URL);
      const data = await response.json();
      if (data) {
        setData(data);
        onFetched(data);
      }
    }

    fetchActivity();
  }, [onFetched]);

  return (
    <p>
      {data?.activity}
    </p>
  );
};

const MyProfile = () => {
  const [data, setData] = useState<Activity | null>(null);

  // Logging the data returned by the child component
  useEffect(() => {
    if (data) {
      console.log(`From child component: ${data.activity}`);
    }
  }, [data]);
```

165

```
    return <MyActivity onFetched={setData} />;
};

export { MyProfile };
```

The MyActivity component fetches an activity from an API within the useEffect callback function. Then, the fetched activity is sent to the parent component via a call to the onFetched callback function that MyActivity receives as a prop.

The MyProfile parent component passed the setData state setter function to the MyActivity component's onFetched prop. When onFetched is called from the MyActivity child component, setData is triggered in the parent component to save the data passed via onFetched to the parent's state.

While this solution does work, it has a serious flaw. The problem with this approach is that the data is flowing upward from child component to parent component. In React, data should always flow downward from the parent component to its child components.

We should remain consistent with the flow of data in a React application. This will makes it easy to find where the data is coming from when we notice an issue with a components. We'll just have to move up the component chain until we find the component that is passing down incorrect data.

The flow of data is very difficult to trace when child components update the state of their parent components using the useEffect Hook.

The main requirement for this example was that both the MyActivity child component and the MyProfile parent component need access to the same data. We can achieve this by allowing the MyProfile parent component fetch that data and then pass it down to the MyActivity child component. Let's implement this improved solution.

```
import { useState, useEffect } from "react";

const API_URL = 'https://www.boredapi.com/api/activity';

type Props = {
  activity: string | null;
};

const MyActivity = ({ activity }: Props) => {
  return (
```

166

```
    <p>
      {activity}
    </p>
  );
};

const MyProfile = () => {
  const [activity, setActivity] = useState<string | null>(null);

  // Good: Fetch data from the parent and pass it to the child
  useEffect(() => {
    async function fetchActivity() {
      const response = await fetch(API_URL);
      const { activity } = await response.json();
      if (activity) {
        setActivity(activity);
      }
    }

    fetchActivity();
  }, []);

  return <MyActivity activity={activity} />;
};

export { MyProfile };
```

We now have a much simpler solution that adheres to the React paradigm of making data flow downward from parent component to child components. This predictable data flow makes our components easier to debug, test, and understand.

useEffect recap

Use effects wisely in React components. With great power comes great responsibility. Using effects incorrectly makes our code harder to understand, slower to run, and more prone to errors.

- `useEffect` cannot be an asynchronous function, but it can invoke asynchronous functions.
- Manage the `useEffect` dependencies array properly to avoid infinite loops.
- `useEffect` can be helpful for fetching data from an API.
- When fetching data within `useEffect`, look out for stale data and race conditions.
- Be sure to clean up side-effects by returning a function from `useEffect`.
- If you can compute it during render, you don't need an effect for it.
- If something needs to be done when a component mounts, use an effect. If not, use event handler functions.
- Don't synchronize state between multiple components with `useEffect`. Lift state up instead.

The useRef hook

The React `useRef` Hook returns a mutable reference, also known as a ref. This ref is an object that can persist across component re-renders. The ref object can be used to store a mutable value, or a reference to a DOM element.

React automatically updates the DOM for us to produce the outputs that we define in our components. As a result, we won't need to manually update the DOM very often.

However, there are times when we will need to access the actual DOM nodes that React manages. We might need to apply focus to a text box, scroll to a specific part of a page, or know a DOM nodes's size and screen coordinates. In React, this is done using a ref to a DOM node.

The `useRef` Hook receives an initial value as a parameter and returns a ref object that has a special `current` property. The `current` property is used to access the value of the ref and to set the value of the ref.

Adding a ref

The first step to adding a ref is importing the React `useRef` Hook into the component.

```
import { useRef } from 'react';
```

We can then make use of the `useRef` Hook inside our component. The only argument that `useRef` receives is the initial value that we want the ref object's `current` property to be initially set to. It can be a value of any type. The initial value is ignored after the initial render.

```
const ref = useRef<number>(0);
```

With TypeScript, we can specify the type of the ref, which we set to `number` here. If we were to output `ref` at this point, we would get the following.

```
{ current: 0 }
```

The `useRef` Hook returns a JavaScript object with one property, called `current`. When we pass nothing to the `useRef` Hook, the value returned for the `current` property will be `undefined`.

We can retrieve the current value of a ref by reading from the ref's `current` property. The `current` property is mutable, meaning that we can write to it directly.

```
const ref = useRef<number>(0);
ref.current = 1;
```

Don't access refs during rendering

During the component render phase, DOM nodes have not been created yet, which means that refs will not be able to reference them yet. During the commit phase, the DOM nodes haven't been updated yet, which means that reading from them won't return accurate results. It's only after the commit phase is complete that React has finished updating the DOM nodes with the corresponding refs.

It's best to avoid accessing refs until after the render and commit phases of a component are complete. This rule of thumb applies whether the refs refer to actual values or to DOM nodes.

Refs are usually accessed from within event handler functions. If there is no particular event handler function available, then refs can be accessed from within the useEffect hook.

useRef versus useState

Let's re-use the Counter component that we used in the section for the useState Hook. Let's update it to use useRef instead of useState. We'll do this in a new component called UseRefCounter.

```
import { useRef } from 'react';

const UseRefCounter = () => {
  const ref = useRef<number>(0);

  const increment = () => {
    ref.current++;
    console.log(`${ref.current} button clicks.`);
  }

  return <button onClick={increment}>{ref.current}</button>
};

export { UseRefCounter };
```

We used the useRef Hook to create a numeric reference that is initialized with a value of 0. When the button is clicked, the increment event handler function is invoked and the current property's value for the ref is incremented. The result is then logged to the console.

If we try running this example, we'll notice that incrementing the value for ref does not trigger a component re-render. This can be seen by the fact that the label for the button, which is set to ref.current, never changes. No matter how many times we click the button, the button label continues to display zero, which is the initial value of the ref that we defined.

Let's now re-visit the Counter component that we saw in the section for the useState Hook. This will allow us to see how useRef and useState are different.

```
import { useState } from 'react';

const Counter = () => {
  const [count, setCount] = useState<number>(0);

  const increment = () => {
    const updatedCount = count + 1;
    console.log(`${updatedCount} button clicks.`);
    setCount(updatedCount);
  }

  return <button onClick={increment}>{count}</button>
};

export { Counter };
```

With the useState Hook, every time the button is clicked, the state is updated and the component re-renders, displaying the incremented value as the button's new label.

The two main differences between the useRef and useState Hooks, or between references and state, are the following:

- Updating a reference doesn't trigger a component re-render, while updating state does.
- Updating a reference is synchronous (the updated reference value is immediately available). Updating state is asynchronous (the updated state value is displayed after the component re-renders).

The reason why updating a ref is synchronous is because a ref is a regular JavaScript object. Refs don't trigger component re-renders when they are set. When we incremented the value for ref.current, React did not re-render the component. This is the opposite of state, which re-renders a component every time state is updated.

The value of ref.current is preserved by React between component re-renders. This is similar to state, which is also preserved by React between re-renders.

Refs

- Do not trigger a component re-render when changed.
- The `current` property of refs can be mutated directly. No immutable updates are needed.
- Avoid reading or writing to the `current` value while the component is rendering.

State

- Triggers a component re-render when updated.
- The state setter function must be used to update state in an immutable way.
- State can be read or written to at any time.

useRef for a stopwatch

Let's use the `useRef` Hook to build a stopwatch. This stopwatch example will demonstrate how refs and state can be used together in the same component. The user will be able to start or stop the stopwatch by pressing the corresponding button.

We'll use the JavaScript `setInterval` function to increase the stopwatch timer by one. The `setInterval` function returns the `id` of the timer. We'll need to reuse this `id` with the JavaScript `clearInterval` function in order to stop the timer. Therefore, we'll store the `id` in a ref called `timerIdRef`.

```
import { useRef, useState, useEffect } from 'react';

const Stopwatch = () => {
  const timerIdRef = useRef<number>(0);
  const [timer, setTimer] = useState<number>(0);

  const startTimer = () => {
    if (timerIdRef.current) {
      return;
    }

    timerIdRef.current = setInterval(() => setTimer((timer) => timer + 1), 10
00);
  };

  const stopTimer = () => {
    clearInterval(timerIdRef.current);
    timerIdRef.current = 0;
  };
```

```
  useEffect(() => {
    return () => clearInterval(timerIdRef.current);
  }, []);

  return (
    <div>
      <p>{timer}</p>
      <div>
        <button onClick={startTimer}>Start</button>
        <button onClick={stopTimer}>Stop</button>
      </div>
    </div>
  );
};

export { Stopwatch };
```

When the "Start" button is clicked, `setInterval` invokes the `setTimer` state setter function after every second to increment the `timer` by 1. The timer id is stored in `timerIdRef`. If `setInterval` is already running when the "Start" button is clicked, we used an early return statement to exit the `startTimer` event handler function, without creating a new timer interval.

When the "Stop" button is clicked, the `clearInterval` function is used to stop the timer by accessing the timer id stored in `timerIdRef`. The timer id stored in `timerIdRef` is then cleared by resetting `timerIdRef.current` to 0.

A `useEffect` Hook was also added in order to define a cleanup function that stops the timer. This way, if the component unmounts while the timer is still running, it will be stopped. We don't need to set `timerIdRef.current` to 0 in the cleanup function because `timerIdRef` will be automatically initialized to zero when the component is mounted again.

In this example, we saw how `useRef` and `useState` can work well together in the same component. The `timer` state was used to track the seconds that have elapsed since the timer started. The ref, that we called `timerIdRef`, was used to save the timer id returned by `setInterval` so that we can stop the timer.

The `useRef` Hook is a better choice than the `useState` hook for tracking the timer id. Remember that refs do not trigger a component re-render when changed.

Component re-renders are already happening every second due to the `setTimer` state setter function being called by `setInterval`. By opting for the `useRef` Hook for the timer id, we avoid introducing more component re-renders every time the "Start" button is clicked. If we had stored the timer `id` in state, every "Start" button click would have produced one more component re-render by a `timerId` state setter function call.

Refs and the DOM

To obtain access to the DOM from a React component, we must to ask React to give us access to a specific DOM node when it renders our component. This is accomplished via a ref.

Since a ref can be assigned any value, we can also use it to access a DOM node. This is a very common reason to use refs. When we pass a ref that we define to a `ref` attribute on an element, such as `<div ref={ref}>`, React will put that corresponding DOM node (the `<div>`) into `ref.current`. We can then manipulate that DOM node via `ref.current`.

To demonstrate this, let's use the `useRef` Hook to programmatically apply focus on an input.

```
import { useRef } from 'react';

const ClickFocus = () => {
  const inputRef = useRef<HTMLInputElement | null>(null);

  const handleClick = () => {
    inputRef.current?.focus();
  }

  return (
    <>
      <input ref={inputRef} type="text" />
      <button onClick={handleClick}>
        Focus
      </button>
    </>
  );
};

export { ClickFocus };
```

Clicking on the "Focus" button will apply focus to the text input.

We used optional chaining on `inputRef.current?.focus()` within the `handleClick()` event handler function. Simply using `inputRef.current.focus()` without the optional chaining for `inputRef.current` causes the line of code to get flagged for an "Object is possibly 'null'." TypeScript error in VS Code. This is because we initialized `inputRef` to be `null`. Thus, TypeScript detects that `inputRef.current` can possibly be `null`.

Using `inputRef.current.focus()` without the optional chaining still makes the example work in the browser. The reason for this is that the `handleClick()` event handler function can only fire once the component has fully rendered. Thus, we can be sure that `inputRef.current` will not be `null` when referenced within this event handler function.

We used `HTMLInputElement | null` when defining `inputRef` with the useRef Hook. This indicates that the `inputRef` could either point to a `null` value or to an `<input />` element. When the component first renders, the DOM node for the input element has not been created yet. Thus, `inputRef` is initialized to `null`. The DOM node for the input element will only be created when the component is done rendering.

useEffect and useRef

What if we want to apply focus on the input immediately when the component loads, without requiring a button click? We can do that as well, but we'll need to use the `useEffect` Hook.

```
import { useRef, useEffect } from 'react';

const InputFocus = () => {
  const inputRef = useRef<HTMLInputElement | null>(null);

  useEffect(() => {
    // HTMLInputElement
    console.log(inputRef.current);

    inputRef.current?.focus();
  }, []);

  // null
  console.log(inputRef.current);

  return <input ref={inputRef} type="text" />;
};

export { InputFocus };
```

When running this example, we'll notice that the `console.log` statement that logs `inputRef.current` directly from the component body, logs a value of `null`. When we access a ref at this point in the component lifecycle, we have no guarantee that the DOM structure has been created yet.

> *We should not access refs during rendering. Refs are set during the commit phase of the React rendering process. Only after the DOM is updated during the commit phase will React refs be set to their corresponding DOM nodes.*

The `useEffect` Hook invokes it's side-effect callback function only after the React component has been mounted to the DOM. Thus, we can be sure that the DOM structure has been created when execution enters the `useEffect` Hook's callback function.

Within the `useEffect` Hook's callback function, the text input has been mounted to the DOM. Thus, we can reference `inputRef.current` without running into a `null` value. Instead, `inputRef` will have it's `current` property set to the DOM node. Referencing `inputRef.current` gives us access to a DOM node of type `HTMLInputElement`.

> *The `useEffect` Hook's callback function is a good place to perform direct DOM manipulations. The DOM structure is guaranteed to have been constructed at this point in the component lifecycle.*

useRef for your own component

When we try to use a ref on one of our own React components, `null` will be returned. Let's try it in at an example. We'll attempt to click on a button to focus the input that is within our own `TextInput` component, but it won't work.

```tsx
import { useRef } from 'react';

const TextInput = () => {
  return <input type="text" />;
}

const TextInputForm = () => {
  const inputRef = useRef<HTMLInputElement | null>(null);

  function handleClick() {
    inputRef.current?.focus();
```

```
  }
  return (
    <>
      <TextInput ref={inputRef} />
      <button onClick={handleClick}>
        Focus Input
      </button>
    </>
  );
};

export { TextInputForm };
```

When coding this example within VS Code, we'll notice that the ref attribute on TextInput gets a red underline. Hovering over the red underline reports the following error.

```
"Property 'ref' does not exist on type 'IntrinsicAttributes'."
```

If we try running the example anyway, we'll get the following error reported in the browser console.

```
"Warning: Function components cannot be given refs. Attempts to access this ref will fail. Did you mean to use React.forwardRef()?"
```

This error occurs because, by default, React intentionally doesn't let a component access the DOM nodes of other components. Thankfully, the error message points us to the solution, and that solution is to use forwardRef.

If we want a React component to expose its DOM nodes, we have to opt in to that behavior by using forwardRef. The forwardRef function allows our React component, TextInput, to "forward" its ref to one of its child elements, input.

```
import { forwardRef, HTMLProps, useRef } from "react";

type TextInputProps = HTMLProps<HTMLInputElement>;

const TextInput = forwardRef<HTMLInputElement, TextInputProps>((props, ref) =
> {
  return <input {...props} ref={ref} />;
});

const TextInputForm = () => {
  const inputRef = useRef<HTMLInputElement | null>(null);

  const handleClick = () => {
```

```
    inputRef.current?.focus();
  }
  return (
    <div>
      <TextInput ref={inputRef} />
      <button onClick={handleClick}>
        Focus Input
      </button>
    </div>
  );
};

export { TextInputForm };
```

By declaring the TextInput component with forwardRef, we have opted in to the component receiving a ref from another component. With forwardRef used on TextInput, the inputRef from TextInputForm can be passed in via the second argument, ref. The TextInput component then passes the ref that it receives to its <input> element.

It's not uncommon to see design system component libraries use forwardRef for low-level React components that are for buttons, inputs, and so forth. They then forward the refs they receive to their DOM nodes.

It's not recommended to have high-level React components exposing their DOM nodes. Doing so can introduce dependencies on the DOM structure and complicate the codebase. Examples of high-level React components would be pages, page sections, forms, lists, etc.

Refs are an escape hatch that cause us to step outside of React. We should use them sparingly. Manually manipulating another component's DOM nodes can make our React code more complex, even if forwardRef is used. Only do it when it's absolutely necessary.

useRef recap

If you need a component to "remember" some information, but you don't want the remembering of that information to trigger a component re-render, use a ref.

A ref is most often used when a React component needs to step outside of React and communicate with external APIs, such as the browser API.

Refs are useful for:

- Storing timer IDs from `setInterval` or `setTimeout`.
- Storing and manipulating DOM nodes.
- Storing values that don't impact the component rendering logic.

If refs are used for non-destructive actions like focusing or scrolling, that's fine. However, too much manual modification of the DOM can risk conflicting with the changes that React makes to the DOM.

Key takeaways for refs:

- Just like state, refs retain information between component re-renders.
- Setting state re-renders a component. Changing a ref's value does not.
- Refs are typically not needed very often.
- Refs are like secret compartments of a component that React doesn't track.
- A ref is a JavaScript object with a single property called `current`, which can be read or set.
- Refs are usually accessed from event handlers. If there is no particular event available, they'll need to be accessed from the `useEffect` Hook.
- Avoid cases where too much of a component's logic relies on refs.

Forms

In React, there are two ways to build forms. We can use a *controlled* component to build the form, or we can use an *uncontrolled* component to build the form.

With controlled components, form data is handled by component state. With uncontrolled components, form data is handled by the DOM. Let's take a look at each approach.

Uncontrolled components

The form fields in uncontrolled components are declared without any component state. The state of uncontrolled fields is managed by the browser rather than by component state.

Refs are used to get the values of the form fields when the form is submitted. The values of form fields are retrieved from their particular DOM node.

Let's take a look at an example of an uncontrolled form that collects the `username` for a user.

```
import { FormEvent, useRef } from "react";

type Props = {
  onSubmit: (username: string) => void;
}

const UserForm = ({ onSubmit }: Props) => {
  const usernameRef = useRef<HTMLInputElement | null>(null);

  const handleSubmit = (event: FormEvent<HTMLFormElement>) => {
    event.preventDefault();

    if (usernameRef.current) {
      onSubmit(usernameRef.current.value);
    }
  };

  return (
    <form onSubmit={handleSubmit}>
      <div>
        <label htmlFor="username">
          Username:
          <input id="username" type="text" ref={usernameRef} />
        </label>
      </div>
```

```
      <button type="submit">Submit</button>
    </form>
  );
};

const UserPage = () => {
  const onSubmit = (username: string) => {
    alert(`Your username is ${username}`);
  }

  return <UserForm onSubmit={onSubmit} />
};

export { UserPage };
```

We used a ref from React's useRef Hook to get the username field's value from the DOM.

Component state is not necessary in uncontrolled forms. Rather than storing the field's value into state every time it changes, we retrieve the field's final value when the form is submitted. Without calls to a state setter function to update state, there is only one render of the UserForm component, the first render.

Let's take a closer look at the code in this example. The handleSubmit event handler receives events of type FormEvent that are triggered by a HTMLFormElement. The handleSubmit event handler calls event.preventDefault to prevent the default behavior of a submit button, thereby preventing a page reload/refresh in the browser.

The ref for the username input field is called usernameRef and we defined it with a type HTMLInputElement | null. This ref will track a HTML input element. This ref will be null when the DOM tree for the component is not yet fully loaded.

We retrieved the current value of the ref by reading from its current property. If the usernameRef.current field is not null, then the onSubmit callback function is called to inform the parent component that the form was submitted. The onSubmit callback function passes along the value of the username input field via usernameRef.current.value.

Uncontrolled fields have their source of truth in the DOM. Since they require no React state, it makes building an uncontrolled form quicker and easier.

If we are building a simple form, using the uncontrolled approach can be a good option. It can also be a good choice for rapidly prototyping a form. For all other cases, it is best to use controlled components for forms, which we'll look at next.

Controlled components

Controlled components use React state to manage form data. The form input fields are bound to state variables, and `onChange` events are used to update the state variables as the user types into the fields.

Let's re-visit the `UserForm` component that we saw above. This time, we'll make it a controlled component instead of an uncontrolled one.

```
import { ChangeEvent, FormEvent, useState } from "react";

type Props = {
  onSubmit: (username: string) => void;
};

const UserForm = ({ onSubmit }: Props) => {
  const [username, setUsername] = useState('');

  const handleSubmit = (event: FormEvent<HTMLFormElement>) => {
    event.preventDefault();
    onSubmit(username);
  };

  const handleChange = (event: ChangeEvent<HTMLInputElement>) => {
    setUsername(event.target.value);
  };

  return (
    <form onSubmit={handleSubmit}>
      <div>
        <label htmlFor="username">
          Username:
          <input
            id="username"
            type="text"
            onChange={handleChange}
            value={username}
          />
        </label>
      </div>
```

```
      <button type="submit">Submit</button>
    </form>
  );
};

const UserPage = () => {
  const onSubmit = (username: string) => {
    alert(`Your username is ${username}`);
  };

  return (
    <div>
      <UserForm onSubmit={onSubmit} />
    </div>
  );
};

export { UserPage };
```

The form data in this example is managed by React state. The useState Hook is used to create a state variable for username. The username state variable is initialized with an empty string because the input field should be empty when the form is first rendered.

The input field for the user's username is bound to a username state variable via the value attribute on the input field. This allows the current value of the state variable to be displayed in the input field.

The onChange attribute on the input field takes what the user typed into it and saves it to the username state via the setUsername state setter function.

When the user submits the form by clicking the "Submit" button, the handleSubmit event handler for the form is called. Inside the handleSubmit function, the default behavior of the form is prevented (which would be to reload the page). Then, the onSubmit callback function is called, passing along the current value of the username state. The parent component, UserPage, is then informed of the username value submitted by the form via its onSubmit callback function.

Recap

- Uncontrolled components are made up of form fields that maintain their own internal state via the DOM, just like a traditional HTML form elements.
- Uncontrolled components read the value of a form element using a ref from the `useRef` Hook.
- In a controlled component, the `value` of the form element is controlled by the component's state.
- When the user interacts with a form element in a controlled component, an event handler updates the state to reflect the new value.
- Controlled components give the component complete control over the values of form elements. They can be used to implement complex form behavior.
- You can mix controlled and uncontrolled form fields in a single form if needed.
- Use controlled components for forms whenever possible.

Custom Hooks

Besides React's built-in Hooks, React allows us to define our own custom Hooks for specific needs of our application. Custom Hooks are like reusable functions but with special rules attached to them.

Before creating our own custom React Hooks, we must know the rules for creating custom Hooks. Besides following the general rules of Hooks in React, custom Hooks must follow two other rules.

- Custom Hooks must always start with the keyword `use` as a prefix, followed by a capital letter, similar to `useState`. An example of a valid custom Hook name is `useLocalStorage`.
- Custom Hooks should make use of built-in React Hooks (`useState`, `useEffect`, etc) or other custom Hooks. This makes a custom Hook a new composition of one or more other Hooks. If a custom Hook doesn't make use of any other Hooks, it shouldn't be a custom Hook.

If a custom Hook does not make use of other Hooks, it's just a reusable function with a name that starts with `use`. By definition, it's not a true custom Hook. However, React won't stop you from creating it and putting code inside it.

Prefixing what is simply a reusable function with `use` can end up confusing other React developers when they see it. It can also cause certain build tools to trigger warnings because the custom Hook naming is used on what is not truly a custom Hook.

The purpose of custom Hooks

React components are like building blocks, and so are Hooks. Hooks are another set of building blocks in our tool box. We can use custom Hooks to combine any number of Hooks in any way that we need.

Custom Hooks allow us to share logic across components. Extracting logic into custom Hooks helps us:

- Reduce code duplication.
- Hide logic from the components that use them.
- Simplify components.

- Simplify refactoring.
- Keep our codebase organized.

Extracting logic and Hooks from components into custom Hooks reduces the code in components. This makes their code more readable, giving us simpler components.

Custom Hooks help us organize logic to make refactoring simpler. Updating the logic in a custom Hook requires updating one file rather than updating what could potentially be many components.

Custom Hooks result in a more organized codebase. When we look at a component's code, we can find its state, effects, and other React features by going to the custom Hooks that it implements.

Custom Hooks help us better understand functions by their name. When we see a function like `getUser` in a component, we know that it won't contain React state or any other Hooks, because its name does not start with the `use` keyword. However, when we see a function with a name like `useLocalStorage`, we know that it will most likely use other Hooks.

Let's consider a `useLocalStorage` custom Hook. What would we find inside this custom Hook? Based on its name, we are likely to find stateful logic that interfaces with the browser's local storage in order to set and get values from it. It's called stateful logic because it reflects the current state of the browser's local storage data structure.

Local storage is key-value data structure that allows web applications to store data locally within the user's browser. The data stored in local storage persists even after the user closes the browser or turns off their device, allowing web applications to remember things like user preferences and more.

Custom Hooks must be pure

The code inside a custom Hook will re-run during every re-render of the component that it lives in. Since custom Hooks re-render together with a component, they can receive the latest props and state values from that component.

Since custom Hooks run during every component render, they must be pure - just like components. This means that given the same inputs, custom Hooks should always return the same outputs.

A custom Hook for a counter

Let's take a look at an example of a custom Hook called useCounter. It manages a state value for a counter. This will allow the counter to be incremented and decremented.

```ts
import { useState } from 'react';

const useCounter = () => {
  const [count, setCount] = useState(0);

  const increment = () => {
    setCount(count => count + 1);
  };

  const decrement = () => {
    setCount(count => count - 1);
  };

  return { count, increment, decrement };
};

export { useCounter };
```

Let's add this custom Hook code to a useCounter.ts file, in a hooks folder. This useCounter custom Hook can now be used in any React component. Let's use it in a Counter component.

```ts
import { useCounter } from './hooks';

const Counter = () => {
  const { count, increment, decrement } = useCounter();

  return (
    <div>
      <p>Count: {count}</p>
      <button onClick={increment}>Increment</button>
      <button onClick={decrement}>Decrement</button>
    </div>
  );
};

export { Counter };
```

Since the state logic for the counter value is in our useCounter custom Hook, our Counter component is quite simple.

Custom Hooks simplify our code, making it more reusable and maintainable. Custom Hooks also promote separation of concerns, separating state logic into its own file. This makes testing our code easier. We can test our custom Hook's state logic separate from the rendering logic in components.

A custom Hook for toggling

Let's take a look at an example of a custom Hook that manages the toggling of a value. This useToggle custom Hook is defined in a useToggle.ts file, in a hooks folder.

```
import { useCallback, useState } from "react";
const useToggle = (initialState: boolean = false): [boolean, () => void] => {
  const [state, setState] = useState(initialState);

  const toggle = useCallback(() => setState(state => !state), []);

  return [state, toggle];
};

export { useToggle };
```

We typed the useToggle custom Hook with a TypeScript tuple of [boolean, () => void]. If we don't explicitly declare the type, we'll end up getting a TypeScript error when trying to use the toggle function from an event handler function in a component.

The reason for this error is because TypeScript infers an array type for the return value of the Hook. As an array, the toggle from [state, toggle] is treated as either boolean or () => void (a function that returns nothing). Without any well-defined order in the [state, toggle] array, state and toggle could be in any array position.

Contrary to an array, a tuple is an array with a fixed size and well-defined data types, allowing us to explicitly declare that toggle in [state, toggle] is of type () => void.

The useToggle custom Hook receives an initialState parameter with value of either true or false and then toggles that value when the toggle function is called. This Hook can be used for opening and closing menus, showing and hiding modals, or showing more text or less text. Any toggling that needs to be done can be done via the useToggle Hook.

Let's use the useToggle custom Hook in a ThemeSwitcher component that toggles between dark mode and light mode.

```
import { useToggle } from './hooks';

const ThemeSwitcher = () => {
  const [isDarkMode, toggleDarkMode] = useToggle(false);
  const theme = isDarkMode ? "dark" : "light";

  return (
    <div className={theme}>
      <p>{theme} mode</p>
      <button onClick={toggleDarkMode}>Toggle Theme</button>
    </div>
  );
};

export { ThemeSwitcher };
```

The useToggle Hook is similar to the useState Hook in that it returns an array where the first element is the state value and the second element is the state updater function. The useToggle custom Hook is just a wrapper for the useState Hook.

In our ThemeSwitcher component, we can name the value and the updater function returned by the useToggle Hook anything we want. It's best to use names that correlate with each other, similar to how we would use the useState Hook. Therefore, we went with isDarkMode and toggleDarkMode. toggleDarkMode references the toggle function in the useToggle Hook.

When the "Toggle Theme" button is clicked, the toggle function from useToggle is triggered, toggling the boolean state value. When isDarkMode is true, the component displays "dark mode" and applies a CSS class named dark. When isDarkMode is false, the component displays "light mode" and applies a CSS class named light.

A custom Hook for localStorage

Let's take a look at another example of a custom Hook that uses the web browser's local storage in order to store a value.

```
import { useState, useEffect, Dispatch, SetStateAction } from 'react';

const useLocalStorage = <T>(key: string, initialValue: T): [T, Dispatch<SetSt
ateAction<T>>] => {
  const [value, setValue] = useState<T>(() => {
    try {
      const storedValue = localStorage.getItem(key);
      return storedValue !== null ? JSON.parse(storedValue) : initialValue;
```

189

```
    } catch (error) {
      return initialValue;
    }
  });

  useEffect(() => {
    localStorage.setItem(key, JSON.stringify(value));
  }, [key, value]);

  return [value, setValue];
};

export { useLocalStorage };
```

The useLocalStorage custom Hook receives two function arguments, a key of type string, and an initialValue of type T. The TypeScript generic type T is used to set the type of the data being stored in local storage. The key represents the local storage key. The initialValue is used as the initial state value if no value is found for the key in local storage.

When the key or value changes, the local storage setItem method stores a JSON-stringified version of value in local storage, indexed by key.

The useState Hook uses a lazy initializer function. This function reads the JSON-stringified value for a certain key in local storage. If the key exists in local storage, it should have a JSON string value associated to it. Therefore, the value is parsed to construct a JavaScript value or object from the JSON string.

The useLocalStorage custom Hook returns an array with two elements: the current value (of type T) and a function to update the value, which takes a parameter of type T.

The useLocalStorage custom Hook helps us simplify the process of reading and writing data to a browser's local storage. This custom Hook can be used in a component to set a value that needs to persist across component re-renders and page refreshes.

Let's take a look at an App component that will use the useLocalStorage Hook to persist the user's theme selection.

```
import { useLocalStorage } from './hooks'

const App = () => {
  const [isDarkTheme, setDarkTheme] = useLocalStorage<boolean>('theme', false
);
```

```
  const toggleTheme = () => setDarkTheme(theme => !theme);

  return (
    <button onClick={toggleTheme}>
      {isDarkTheme ? `Dark` : `Light`} Theme
    </button>
  );
};

export { App };
```

The generic type T of the `useLocalStorage` Hook is set to `boolean`, indicating that the type of the data being stored and retrieved from local storage is of type `boolean`.

The `useLocalStorage` Hook is essentially a wrapper for the `useState` Hook that is used internally. `isDarkTheme` refers to the state value, and `setDarkTheme` refers to the state setter function. The initial value passed to `useLocalStorage` is `false`, making the light theme the initial theme.

Clicking on the button calls the `toggleTheme` function. It uses the `setDarkTheme` state setter function from the `useLocalStorage` Hook to toggle the theme. The currently toggled theme is persisted to the browser's local storage by the `useLocalStorage` Hook. If we refresh the page, or close the page and then re-visit it, our last theme selection is remembered and displayed.

A custom Hook for fetching data

In the section about the `useEffect` Hook, we learned that client-side data fetching is typically done via effects. Custom Hooks can help us to better organize our data fetching logic. Custom Hooks allow us to extract data fetching logic out of our components.

Let's take a look at a custom Hook called `useData` for client-side data fetching.

```
import { useEffect, useState } from "react";

const useData = <T>(url: string) => {
  const [data, setData] = useState<T | null>(null);
  const [loading, setLoading] = useState<boolean>(false);
  const [error, setError] = useState<boolean>(false);

  useEffect(() => {
    if (url) {
      let ignore = false;
```

```
    const fetchData = async () => {
      setLoading(true);
      try {
        const response = await fetch(url);
        const data = await response.json();
        if (!ignore) {
          setData(data);
          setLoading(false);
        }
      } catch (error) {
        setError(true);
        setLoading(false);
      }
    };

    fetchData();

    return () => {
      ignore = true;
    };
  }
}, [url]);

  return { data, loading, error };
};

export { useData };
```

The data fetching logic used in the `useData` Hook is nothing new. We've already seen it in the section about the `useEffect` Hook. The only difference here is that the data fetching logic is isolated into a custom Hook rather than being embedded directly in a component.

The TypeScript generic type T is used on the `useData` Hook so that we can specify the type of the `data` that we're fetching.

The `useData` Hook receives a `url` that it will use to fetch data from. State variables for `loading` and `error` were added to the `useData` Hook so that we can inform components when a request is loading and when a request fails.

The `ignore` variable and the `useEffect` cleanup function are used to handle potential race conditions by ignoring stale responses. When there are multiple simultaneous requests for data via our custom Hook, all responses except the one for the last request will be ignored.

Let's use the `useData` custom Hook in a `MyActivity` component that will fetch and display a random activity.

```
import { useData } from './hooks';

const API_URL = 'https://www.boredapi.com/api/activity';

type Activity = {
  activity: string;
};

const MyActivity = () => {
  const { data, loading, error } = useData<Activity>(API_URL);

  if (loading) {
    return <p>Loading...</p>;
  }

  return (
    <>
      <h4>Activity</h4>
      {loading && <p>Loading...</p>}
      {error && <p>An error occurred.</p>}
      {data && <p>{data.activity}</p>}
    </>
  );
};

export { MyActivity };
```

We defined the type of the data that the `MyActivity` component fetches using the `Activity` type. We used the `Activity` type to configure the generic T type of the `useData` Hook.

Extracting all the data fetching logic into a custom Hook makes requesting data at the component level very simple. All we had to do to fetch data was to import `useData` and pass it a URL to fetch data from.

The `useData` custom Hook can be used in any component that needs to fetch data from an API. It's also possible to use `useData` several times in the same component in order to fetch data from more than one API endpoint.

When we load a page that uses the `MyActivity` component, a random activity will be displayed. If we have a good internet connection, the fetch request for the `MyActivity` component happens very quickly. This causes the "Loading…" indicator to only be displayed for a few milliseconds. In order to really notice the "Loading…" indicator, we may have to refresh the page a few times.

Custom Hooks do not share state

Custom Hooks do not share state. Using the same custom Hook multiple times does not share any state between each usage of that Hook. This is true whether the custom Hook is used multiple times in the same component or across several components.

The state and effects inside a custom Hook are fully isolated. This means that every call to a custom Hook gets its own isolated state.

Let's take a look at an example to prove this point. This example consists of a form that prompts a user for their first and last name, and then greets them. For demonstration purposes, we'll extract the `useState` logic to a custom Hook called `useFormField`. We'll then use the `useFormField` custom Hook multiple times in the same component to show that no state is shared between them.

```
import { ChangeEvent, useState } from 'react';

const UserForm = () => {
  const [firstName, setFirstName] = useState('');
  const [lastName, setLastName] = useState('');

  const handleFirstNameChange = (e: ChangeEvent<HTMLInputElement>) => {
    setFirstName(e.target.value);
  };

  const handleLastNameChange = (e: ChangeEvent<HTMLInputElement>) => {
    setLastName(e.target.value);
  };

  return (
    <>
      <label>
        First name:
        <input value={firstName} onChange={handleFirstNameChange} />
      </label>
      <label>
        Last name:
        <input value={lastName} onChange={handleLastNameChange} />
      </label>

      {(firstName && lastName) &&
        <p>Hello, {firstName} {lastName}.</p>
```

```
      }
    </>
  );
};

export { UserForm };
```

Typing in a first name and a last name in the respective text inputs will update the state for `firstName` and `lastName`, and display a greeting.

The `UserForm` component actually contains repetitive logic for each form field. The repetitive logic consists of:

- The state variables (`firstName` and `lastName`).
- The onChange handler functions (`handleFirstNameChange` and `handleLastNameChange`).
- The JSX that sets the `value` and `onChange` attributes for the input elements.

We can extract this repetitive logic into a `useFormField` custom Hook that we'll define in a `useFormField.ts` file, in a hooks folder.

```
import { ChangeEvent, useState } from 'react';

const useFormField = (initialValue: string) => {
  const [value, setValue] = useState(initialValue);

  const onChange = (event: ChangeEvent<HTMLInputElement>) => {
    setValue(event.target.value);
  }

  return {
    value,
    onChange
  };
};

export { useFormField };
```

With the repetitive form field logic now extracted into the `useFormField` custom Hook, we can now use it in the `UserForm` component.

```
import { useFormField } from './hooks';

const UserForm = () => {
  const firstNameProps = useFormField('');
  const lastNameProps = useFormField('');
```

```
  return (
    <>
      <label>
        First name:
        <input {...firstNameProps} />
      </label>
      <label>
        Last name:
        <input {...lastNameProps} />
      </label>

      {(firstNameProps.value && lastNameProps.value) &&
        <p>Hello, {firstNameProps.value} {lastNameProps.value}.</p>
      }
    </>
  );
};

export { UserForm };
```

The `useFormField` Hook only declares one internal state variable called `value`. The `UserForm` component calls the `useFormField` Hook twice, but each time, it refers to a different state value.

We can confirm this by typing different values for the first name and the last name. Rather than seeing the same value displayed in both text inputs, we see the different first name and last name values that we typed in each input.

Therefore, using a custom Hook multiple times is just like declaring separate state variables. No state is shared when a custom Hook like `useFormField` is used multiple times in the same component.

Custom Hooks only allow us to share stateful logic, but not state itself. Every single usage of a custom Hook has completely independent state variables and effects.

When to use custom Hooks

When we have component logic that makes use of Hooks, and when that logic also needs to be used by other components, we should extract that logic into a custom Hook.

We shouldn't create custom Hooks for every duplication of code that we find. Some code duplication is acceptable. In a real application, the `useFormField` Hook that we created above may not really be necessary, since it wraps just one `useState` Hook.

Whenever we write a `useEffect` Hook, we should consider moving it to a custom Hook. We should not need to use the `useEffect` Hook very often. However, when `useEffect` is needed, wrapping it into a custom Hook is ideal.

By moving effects into custom Hooks, it isolates effects logic, improves the organization of effects, and simplifies components. Other developers who may end up working on our components will be less likely to accidentally break any effects logic, since that logic is isolated in its own Hook and its own file.

When an effect is wrapped in a custom Hook, we can be more precise in communicating its responsibility with the naming of the custom Hook. We can give that effect a specific name, rather than embedding it into a generic `useEffect` Hook - which makes that logic hard to find later.

Custom Hooks from the community

There are many great custom Hook libraries maintained by the React community. The most recommended Hook libraries are **usehooks-ts** (https://usehooks-ts.com), **useHooks** (https://usehooks.com), and **React Use** (https://github.com/streamich/react-use).

Browsing these Hook libraries is helpful for learning Hooks. They can be copy-pasted as needed into your next project.

Recap

- Custom Hooks must always start with the keyword `use` as a prefix, followed by a capital letter.
- Custom Hooks should make use of built-in React Hooks or other custom Hooks.
- Custom Hooks should be pure because they run during every component render.
- Extracting logic into custom Hooks helps us to reduce code duplication, simplify our components, and better organize our codebase.
- Custom Hooks do not share state. Custom Hooks allow us to share stateful logic, but not state itself.
- Abstracting effects behind a custom Hook allows us to give them a more readable name.
- We should aim to have most of our application's effects in custom Hooks.

Performance Hooks

As React applications grow in complexity, the number of components and the frequency of component renders can have a significant impact on performance.

To address performance issues, React provides several performance optimization techniques, including the use of advanced Hooks such as `useMemo` and `useCallback`. These Hooks allow developers to memoize values and functions, reducing the number of unnecessary re-renders and improving overall application performance.

React also provides the `memo` higher-order component (HOC) to memoize a component, which means that the component will only re-render when its props have changed. It's useful for preventing unnecessary re-renders of a component.

> *A higher-order component (HOC) is a function that receives a component and returns a new component with extended functionality.*

The `useMemo` Hook is used to memoize a value or computation, which means that the value is only calculated when necessary. This Hook is useful for expensive calculations or computations that only need to be performed once.

The `useCallback` Hook is used to memoize a function, which means that the function is only recreated when its dependencies have changed. This Hook is useful for preventing unnecessary re-renders of a component that depends on a function as a prop.

The last two performance Hooks that we'll look at in this section are the `useTransition` and `useDeferredValue` Hooks. These two Hooks make use of React's concurrent rendering to help us build more fluid user experiences in our apps.

By the end of this section, you will have a solid understanding of how to use `useMemo`, `memo`, `useCallback`, `useTransition`, and `useDeferredValue` to improve the performance of your React applications.

The useMemo Hook

The `useMemo` Hook is used to *remember* a computed value between component renders, which means that the value is only calculated when necessary. This Hook is useful for expensive calculations or computations that only need to be performed once.

React uses something called a *re-render* to keep our application's user interface in sync with the state of our application. Think of each re-render as a snapshot in time. Each snapshot holds what our application's user interface looks like, based on the application state at that time.

Every time React re-renders, React creates a new snapshot, compares it with previous snapshots, and automatically figures out which DOM nodes need to change. React is optimized for performance out of the box, which means that we usually don't have to worry about re-renders.

However, there are situations where React's snapshot creation during re-renders can take a while. This is problematic because it results in a user interface that is slow to update after a user performs an action on the screen.

Memoization

The `useMemo` and `useCallback` Hooks are performance-related React Hooks. They both help with optimizing component re-renders. Both of these Hooks use *memoization* to improve the performance of components.

Memoization is an optimization technique that caches a computed result. The next time that computed result is needed, it is retrieved from the cache rather than being re-computed again. A cache is just a temporary storage that holds data so that future requests for that data can be served faster.

The `useMemo` and `useCallback` Hooks reduce:

- The amount of computations that need to be done during a given component render.
- The number of times that a component needs to re-render.

Using useMemo

The `useMemo` Hook accepts 2 arguments - a function that computes a result, and an array of dependencies. Think of `useMemo` like a cache, and the dependencies are the cache invalidation strategy.

```
const memoizedResult = useMemo(expensiveFunction, dependencies);
```

The function that is wrapped in `useMemo` should be a pure function. A pure function only performs a calculation and nothing more. Given the same input(s), a pure function will always return the same output.

During the first component render, the `useMemo` Hook will invoke the function named `expensiveFunction`, memoize the result, and return it to the component-level variable `memoizedResult`.

If no dependencies array is provided for the `useMemo` Hook, it will compute a new value on every component render. This will not result in any performance improvements and defeat the purpose of using `useMemo`. Therefore, be sure to specify a dependencies array.

Let's take a more in-depth look at the dependencies array for the `useMemo` Hook.

```
const memoizedResult = useMemo(() => {
  return expensiveFunction(dependencyA, dependencyB);
}, [dependencyA, dependencyB]);
```

The `expensiveFunction` depends on two values that could either be from component props or component state. As a result, we added the two variables that `expensiveFunction` depends on to the dependencies array of the `useMemo` Hook.

The above `useMemo` invocation will run during the component's initial render, invoke `expensiveFunction` with the initial values of the dependencies, memoize the result, and store that result in the component's `memoizedResult` variable.

If the values of the dependencies don't change during component re-renders, then `useMemo` will not invoke `expensiveFunction` again. Instead, it will return the memoized value.

If the values of the dependencies do change during component re-renders, then `useMemo` will re-invoke `expensiveFunction` with the new values for the variables in the dependencies array. The new result will be memoized and stored in the component's `memoizedResult` variable.

A factorial function

Let's take a look at a `Factorial` component that calculates the factorial of a number. This component uses a `getFactorial` function to compute the factorial of a number.

We will notice that every time the `Factorial` component re-renders, the `getFactorial` function will run and re-compute the factorial for the same number. These re-computations are unnecessary and can become a performance bottleneck. Let's look at how the `useMemo` Hook solve this issue.

```
import { ChangeEvent, useState } from 'react';

const getFactorial = (value: number): number => {
  console.log('getFactorial called...');

  return value <= 0 ? 1 : value * getFactorial(value - 1);
};

const Factorial = () => {
  const [number, setNumber] = useState(1);
  const [counter, setCounter] = useState(0);
  const factorial = getFactorial(number);

  const onChange = (event: ChangeEvent<HTMLInputElement>) => {
    setNumber(Number(event.target.value));
  };

  const onClick = () => {
    console.log('Re-rendering component...');
    setCounter(counter => counter + 1);
  }

  return (
    <div>
      <p>
        The factorial of
        <input
          type="text"
          value={number}
          onChange={onChange} /> is {factorial}.
      </p>
      <button onClick={onClick}>Re-render component</button>
    </div>
  );
};

export { Factorial };
```

Every time the user changes the value of the text input in the Factorial component, the factorial is computed and the message, "getFactorial called...", is logged to the console.

The problem arises when the user clicks on the "Re-render component" button. When this button is clicked, the message "getFactorial called..." is also logged to the console. This is because a side-effect of re-rendering the component is that the getFactorial function re-computes the factorial of the current number.

Since the component has already computed the factorial of the current number when it was first entered in the text input, we don't need to re-compute the same factorial value for us when the component re-renders. This is where memoization can help.

We can use the useMemo Hook on the getFactorial function call, so that it remembers the computed factorial value between component re-renders and does not re-compute it. Let's make this change to the Factorial component.

```
import { ChangeEvent, useState } from 'react';

const getFactorial = (value: number): number => {
  console.log('getFactorial called...');

  return value <= 0 ? 1 : value * getFactorial(value - 1);
};

const Factorial = () => {
  const [number, setNumber] = useState(1);
  const [counter, setCounter] = useState(0);
  // Good: memoize the computed factorial value
  const factorial = useMemo(() => getFactorial(number), [number]);

  const onChange = (event: ChangeEvent<HTMLInputElement>) => {
    setNumber(Number(event.target.value));
  };

  const onClick = () => {
    console.log('Re-rendering component...');
    setCounter(counter => counter + 1);
  }

  return (
    <div>
      <p>
        The factorial of
        <input
```

```
        type="text"
        value={number}
        onChange={onChange} /> is {factorial}.
    </p>
    <button onClick={onClick}>Re-render component</button>
   </div>
  );
};

export { Factorial };
```

Every time the user changes the value of the text input, the message "getFactorial called..." is still logged to the console. This is expected. The `useMemo` Hook has not done anything to change this expected behavior.

The benefit of `useMemo` can be seen when clicking on the "Re-render component" button. The message "getFactorial called..." is no longer logged to the console.

If the `number` state variable holds the same value that it did during the previous component render, `useMemo` returns the last computed result that it memoized, without re-computing anything.

The `useMemo` Hook will only re-run the `getFactorial` function when the `number` state variable changes. This is because the `number` state variable is included in the dependencies array of the `useMemo` Hook. The reason why we added the `number` state variable to the dependencies array is because the `getFactorial` function depends on it as a required function parameter.

A product filtering function

Let's apply the `useMemo` Hook to a more complex example. This example consists of displaying a filtered list of products, and the ability to start and stop a sale of products.

Let's first take a look at the `Products` component.

```
import { useState } from 'react';
import { getProducts } from './utils';

const products = getProducts();

const Products = () => {
  const [tab, setTab] = useState('all');
  const [isSale, setIsSale] = useState(false);

  return (
    <>
```

```
      <button onClick={() => setTab('all')}>
        All
      </button>
      <button onClick={() => setTab('available')}>
        Available
      </button>
      <button onClick={() => setTab('sold')}>
        Sold
      </button>

      <hr />

      <div>
        <button onClick={() => setIsSale(isSale => !isSale)}>
          {isSale ? 'Stop' : 'Start'} Sale
        </button>
      </div>

      <hr />

      <ProductList
        products={products}
        tab={tab}
        isSale={isSale}
      />
    </>
  );
};

export { Products };
```

The `Products` component uses the `getProducts` function to get an array of products that are passed to the `ProductList` component. The `getProducts` function, imported from the `utils.ts` file, generates a random list of products.

The `Products` component displays three tabs: "All", "Available", and "Sold". Below the tabs is a button that the user can press to start or stop a sale. Below the sale button, the `ProductList` component is used to display a list of products.

Let's take a look at the `ProductList` component.

```
import { useMemo } from 'react';
import { filterProducts, Product } from './utils';

type Props = {
  products: Product[];
  tab: string;
```

```
    isSale: boolean;
};

const ProductList = ({ products, tab, isSale }: Props) => {
  const filteredProducts = useMemo(
    () => filterProducts(products, tab),
    [products, tab]
  );

  return (
    <>
      {isSale &&
        <p>Products sale is on!</p>
      }

      <ul>
        {filteredProducts.map(product => (
          <li key={product.id}>
            {product.isSold ?
              <s>{product.name}</s> :
              product.name
            }
          </li>
        ))}
      </ul>
    </>
  );
};

export { ProductList };
```

The ProductList component receives a list of products, the name of the currently active tab, and the sale status. The ProductList component makes a call to a filterProducts function that filters the array of products based on the currently active tab.

The call to the filterProducts function is wrapped in a useMemo Hook. The products array and the current tab are added to the dependencies array of useMemo. This will cause the filtered products to be re-computed only when the products array changes or the current tab changes. If neither change, then the last filtered products list will remain memoized in the filteredProducts variable.

Let's take a look at the filterProducts function that is imported from the utils.ts file.

```
const filterProducts = (products: Product[], tab: string): Product[] => {
  console.log(`Filtering ${products.length} products for tab ${tab}.`);
```

```
  const startTime = performance.now();
  while (performance.now() - startTime < 500) {
    // simulate expensive code
    // wait 500 ms
  };

  return products.filter(product => {
    if (tab === 'all') {
      return true;
    } else if (tab === 'available') {
      return !product.isSold;
    } else if (tab === 'sold') {
      return product.isSold;
    }
  });
};
```

The filterProducts function implements a 500 millisecond delay to simulate a slow and expensive function that merits the use of the useMemo Hook.

When we click on a tab, the response will feel slow because the filterProducts function, with its artificial delay, has to re-run. The tab is in the dependencies array of the useMemo Hook. Therefore, a change in tab will re-run the filterProducts function.

When we click on the "Start Sale" button in the Products component, it will feel fast. A "Products sale is on!" message will be displayed by the ProductList component. When the sale is active, clicking the "Stop Sale" button will remove the sale message.

The artificial delay added to filterProducts will not affect the starting and stopping of the sale. This is thanks to the useMemo Hook used in the ProductList component. When we click on the sale button, the filterProducts function call is skipped because both the products array and the current tab, the useMemo dependencies, have not changed since the last render.

Now, let's remove the useMemo Hook that is used in the ProductList component and see how performance is affected.

```
const filteredProducts = filterProducts(products, tab);
```

When we click on the sale button, to start or stop a sale, it feels slow now. While it was quick when useMemo was used, there is now a noticeable delay. It suffers from the same artificial delay that changing tabs suffers from.

This issue occurs because the `filterProducts` function, with its artificial delay, is now getting called every time the sale button in the `Products` component is clicked. With each click of the sale button, the `isSale` state is updated, triggering a component re-render that also re-renders the `ProductList` child component with a new value for its `isSale` prop.

With no `useMemo` Hook in place to optimize calls to `filterProducts`, the function now gets called even when the `products` array and the current `tab` have not changed.

If no artificial delay was added to `filterProducts`, then it may have been fine to use it without `useMemo`. However, we introduced this artificial delay in order to show that when a function is slow because it operates on a lot of items, it's best to optimize it with `useMemo`. The `useMemo` Hook prevents the expensive function from needlessly re-running when some unrelated state variable changed.

When to use useMemo

Most of the time, React code without any memoization applied to it works fine. If the application responds quickly enough to user requests without `useMemo`, then we may not need to apply memoization.

The `useMemo` Hook is simply a performance optimization. If the code doesn't work without the `useMemo` Hook, it won't work with the `useMemo` Hook. The underlying problem in the code will need to be fixed first.

It's not advised to use the `useMemo` Hook to memoize every computed value. While there may not be any harm in that, it makes our code look more complex than it should. Applying memoization to a value that needs to be re-computed frequently makes memoization and `useMemo` useless.

Optimizing with the `useMemo` Hook is only recommended when computing a value is noticeably slow, and the dependencies of that computation don't change very often.

useMemo recap

- The useMemo Hook is a performance optimization for cases where computing a value is computationally expensive, and thus, noticeably slow.
- The useMemo Hook memoizes the value computed by a function so that the value does not get re-computed on every component render.
- If the dependencies of useMemo don't change during component re-renders, then useMemo will return the memoized value.
- If the dependencies of useMemo do change during component re-renders, then useMemo will re-invoke the provided function and memoize its return value.
- The function that is wrapped in useMemo should be a pure function.
- Over-using useMemo can cause performance degradation rather than performance optimization.
- Using useMemo to memoize a value that frequently needs to be re-computed defeats the purpose of memoization.

memo

In order to fully understand the next React Hook that we'll be looking at, the `useCallback` Hook, it's important to first understand `memo`.

React provides a higher-order component, called `memo`, that wraps around a component to memoize the rendered output of that component and avoid unnecessary re-renders.

`memo` allows us to skip re-rendering a component when its props have not changed. The usual behavior of a React component is that it re-renders when any of its props change. `memo` memoizes the component to avoid re-rendering it when none of its props have changed.

Using memo

Using `memo` is as simple as wrapping a React component with it.

```
import { memo } from 'react';

const Product = () => {
  // ...
};

const ProductMemoized = memo(Product);

export { ProductMemoized };
```

`memo` does not modify the `Product` component. Instead, it returns a new, memoized version of the component. In the above example, `ProductMemoized` is a component that behaves exactly like the `Product` component. The only difference between the two is that `ProductMemoized` will only be re-rendered if the `Product` props have changed. On the other hand, the `Product` component will always be re-rendered whenever it's parent component re-renders.

memo in action

Let's define a `Book` component that renders details about a book. We'll wrap this component in `memo` and assign it to `MemoizedBook`.

```
import { memo } from 'react';

type Props = {
  title: string;
  author: string;
```

```
};

const Book = ({ title, author }: Props) => {
  return (
    <>
      <p>{title} by {author}</p>
    </>
  );
};

const MemoizedBook = memo(Book);
```

The invocation of memo(Book) returns a new, memoized component that we have named MemoizedBook. MemoizedBook renders the same content as the original Book component. The only difference is that MemoizedBook is a memoized version of Book.

When using MemoizedBook instead of Book, if the props title and author do not change between re-renders, React will reuse the memoized component instead of rendering a new one. All unnecessary re-renders of the Book component are skipped when we use MemoizedBook, thanks to memo.

Let's look at an example of a Books component that makes use of both MemoizedBook and Book components. The Books component will have a button that, when clicked, will re-render itself. This will allow us to see the difference that memo makes.

```
import { useState, useEffect } from "react";
import { memo } from 'react';

type Props = {
  title: string;
  author: string;
  isMemoized: boolean;
};

const Book = ({ title, author, isMemoized }: Props) => {
  console.log(
    `${isMemoized ? "<MemoizedBook>" : "<Book>"} rendered for ${title}.`
  );

  return (
    <>
      <p>{title} by {author}</p>
    </>
  );
};
```

```
const MemoizedBook = memo(Book);

const Books = () => {
  // this state is used to re-render Books
  const [, setClicks] = useState<number>(0);

  return (
    <>
      <button onClick={() => setClicks(clicks => clicks += 1)}>Re-render</button>
      <MemoizedBook
        title="Book A"
        author="Author A"
        isMemoized={true} />

      <Book
        title="Book B"
        author="Author B"
        isMemoized={false} />
    </>
  );
};

export { Books };
```

When trying out this example, we'll need to pay attention to the browser console to see what messages get logged.

Every time the "Re-render" button is clicked, the message "`<Book> rendered for Book B.`" is logged to the console, but no message is logged to the console for "Book A". This is because "Book A" is rendered with `MemoizedBook` while "Book B" is rendered with Book.

As long as the `title` and `author` props for `MemoizedBook` do not change, it will not re-render.

When to use memo

If a component isn't computationally expensive and its props change often, then it probably does not need `memo`.

If a component with frequently changing props is wrapped with `memo`, performance won't be optimized. In fact, performance may even get worse. This is because React will end up having to do extra work. The extra work is in the fact that React has to needlessly run a comparison function to determine if the component's previous and current props are the same or not. Thus, if the component's props change often, memo is counterproductive.

If we cannot quantify the performance gains of memoizing a component, or point to a noticeable difference, then we probably don't need memo. When we apply performance optimizations needlessly, we risk degrading performance.

memo recap

- Wrap a component with memo to get a memoized version of that component.
- If the props of the component wrapped with memo haven't changed, that component will not be re-rendered when its parent component is re-rendered.
- If a component isn't computationally expensive and its props change often, don't use memo.
- If memo is used on a component with frequently changing props, performance may actually degrade rather than improve.

The useCallback Hook

The React `useCallback` Hook is very similar to the `useMemo` Hook. They both achieve the same thing, performance optimizations via memoization (caching). The only difference with the `useCallback` Hook is that it memoizes functions rather than values returned by functions.

Using useCallback

The `useCallback` Hook is added to the top level of a component in order to memoize a function between component re-renders.

Just like `useMemo`, the `useCallback` Hook accepts two arguments - a function that computes a result, and an array of dependencies. Think of `useCallback` as a cache for a function reference, and the dependencies are the cache invalidation strategy.

```
const memoizedResult = useCallback(someFunction, dependencies);
```

`someFunction` is the function that we want to memoize. This function can take any arguments. The `dependencies` array is an optional second argument. It is used to specify the values that the memoized function depends on. The dependencies array can include props, state, or variables declared in the component.

During the first component render, `useCallback` will return a memoized reference for the function that we provided to it. The `useCallback` Hook will not call the function. It's up to us to decide when and where to call the function.

React compares the current values of the `dependencies` with their values from the previous render, to see if any have changed. When any value in the `dependencies` array changes, the memoized function provided to `useCallback` will be re-created. As a result, `useCallback` will return a new function reference in memory. The memoized function is re-created so that it can update its computations due to the changes to its dependencies.

If the `dependencies` for `useCallback` have not changed, then `useCallback` will return the same function reference.

If the `dependencies` array is omitted from `useCallback`, the memoized function will never be re-created. This can be problematic if the function depends on changing values beyond its scope.

Memoizing functions

When optimizing the rendering performance of React components, we sometimes need to memoize the functions that we pass to child components.

In JavaScript, functions are objects. Functions can be passed to other functions, returned by other functions, and assigned to variables. Functions can also have properties and methods just like objects can. The only thing that distinguishes JavaScript functions from other JavaScript objects is that functions can be called.

Just like JavaScript objects, functions in JavaScript are compared by reference, not by value. To demonstrate this, let's use a JavaScript strict equality check to compare two functions that return the same value.

```
const firstFunction = () => {
  return 1;
};

const secondFunction = () => {
  return 1;
};

console.log(firstFunction === secondFunction); // false
```

Though both functions return the same value, the strict equality comparison of both functions returns `false`.

When we define a function within a React component, that function will be re-created on every component re-render. It's the same function being re-created, however, each time it is re-created it receives a unique reference in memory.

```
const SomeComponent = () => {
  // function re-created on every component re-render
  const handleClick = () => {
    console.log('Clicked.');
  };

  // ...
};

export { SomeComponent };
```

In the code above, the `handleClick` function will be re-created on every re-render of `SomeComponent`. Each time that `handleClick` is re-created, it will be assigned a unique memory reference.

Let's add `useCallback` to the `handleClick` function and see what happens.

```
import { useCallback } from 'react';

const SomeComponent = () => {
  // the function reference is cached
  const handleClick = useCallback(() => {
    console.log('Clicked!');
  }, []);

  // ...
};

export { SomeComponent };
```

In this case, the `handleClick` variable will always receive the same function instance with the same memory reference, even if `SomeComponent` re-renders many times.

Functions like `handleClick` are not computationally expensive. The re-creation of such functions on every component re-render is usually not a problem. Having a few functions like `handleClick` declared within our React components is perfectly normal. Most simple functions like `handleClick` don't usually require `useCallback` for performance optimizations. We added `useCallback` to this basic example only for demonstration purposes.

There are cases where we need to maintain a single function reference between component re-renders. Let's take a look at two of the most common cases below.

The useCallback Hook for memo

When a function is passed as a prop to a component wrapped in memo, the `useCallback` Hook is needed

When a component re-renders, the functions in that component are re-created. If a function is passed via props to a component wrapped with memo, and a re-render occurs, memo will think that the prop with the function has changed. However, it didn't really change. The function was simply re-created as part of the normal component re-rendering process. The result is that component memoization will not occur, and we'll end up losing the performance benefit of memo.

Let's take a look at an example of this scenario. The solution will be to use the `useCallback` Hook.

```
import { memo, useState } from 'react';

const getBooks = () => {
  return [{ title: 'Book A' }, { title: 'Book B' }, { title: 'Book C' }];
};

type BooksProps = {
  searchTerm: string;
  onClick: (title: string) => void;
};

const Books = ({ searchTerm, onClick }: BooksProps) => {
  console.log(`Books list rendered. searchTerm is ${searchTerm}.`);

  // this getBooks() call could be expensive
  const books = getBooks();

  const booksList = books.map(({ title }) => {
    const hasMatch = title === searchTerm;
    return (
      <li
        key={title}
        onClick={() => onClick(title)}
        style={{ color: hasMatch ? 'green' : 'black' }}>{title}</li>
    );
  });

  return (
    <ul>
      {booksList}
    </ul>
  );
};

const MemoizedBooks = memo(Books);

type CatalogProps = {
  searchTerm: string;
};

const Catalog = ({ searchTerm }: CatalogProps) => {
  // Bad: this function breaks the memoization of `MemoizedBooks`
  const onClick = (title: string) => {
    console.log(`You clicked ${title}`);
  };
```

216

```
  return (
    <>
      <MemoizedBooks
        searchTerm={searchTerm}
        onClick={onClick} />
    </>
  );
};

const App = () => {
  const [searchTerm, setSearchTerm] = useState('');
  // used to re-render this component
  const [, setClicks] = useState(0);

  return (
    <>
      <div>
        <input type="text" value={searchTerm} onChange={(event) => setSearchTerm(event.target.value)} />
      </div>
      <div>
        <button onClick={() => setClicks(clicks => clicks += 1)}>Re-render</button>
      </div>
      <Catalog searchTerm={searchTerm} />
    </>
  );
};

export { App };
```

In the example above, `memo` is used to wrap a `Books` component in order to create a `MemoizedBooks` component. `memo` is needed because the `Books` component makes a call to a `getBooks` function, which could be computationally expensive, returning thousands of book results. Therefore, we should memoize this component so that it doesn't re-render when its props haven't changed.

The `MemoizedBooks` component is a child component of the `Catalog` component. The `Catalog` component passes a `searchTerm` and an `onClick` function as props to its child component, `MemoizedBooks`.

The App component makes use of the `Catalog` component to show a list of books. The App component also provides a text input so that users can find a book by its title. Every change to the text input re-renders the App component and all of its children. The App component also has a "Re-render" button that, when pressed, re-renders the App component and all of its children.

The problem with this example is that clicking on the "Re-render" button in the App component keeps on re-rendering the MemoizedBooks component. This is noticeable because the message, "Books list rendered. searchTerm is .", keeps getting logged to the console every time the "Re-render" button is clicked. No search term is included in the logged message because searchTerm is initialized as an empty string.

The fact that we see this message on every button click means that the MemoizedBooks component is being re-rendered every time. Since MemoizedBooks is memoized using memo, and none of its props have changed, it should not be re-rendering.

The cause of this problem is the onClick function, which is passed as a prop to MemoizedBooks from the Catalog component. The Catalog component re-renders every time the "Re-render" button is clicked in the App component. As a result, the onClick function, defined in Catalog, gets re-created on every component re-render. This causes the onClick prop for MemoizedBooks to receive a new function with every re-render, breaking the component memoization of memo.

We can fix this issue by wrapping the onClick function with the useCallback Hook.

```
const onClick = useCallback((title: string) => {
  console.log(`You clicked ${title}`);
}, [searchTerm]);
```

The searchTerm was added to the dependencies array of useCallback. If the searchTerm has not changed, we don't want to re-render the MemoizedBooks component. However, if the searchTerm does change, we want to re-render MemoizedBooks because it logs the searchTerm to the console and changes the color of any matching book titles.

After adding the useCallback Hook to the onClick function, clicking the "Re-render" button no longer re-renders the MemoizedBooks component. The App component still re-renders because clicking the button updates its local state. The Catalog component also still re-renders because it's a child of the App component. However, MemoizedBooks does not get re-rendered.

When the value of searchTerm has not changed between component re-renders, useCallback returns a memoized version of the onClick function. The onClick function is no

218

longer re-created on every re-render of the `Catalog` component. The `onClick` function only gets re-created when `searchTerm` changes in value.

We also have the option to define the function passed to `useCallback` outside of the Hook. Here's what that would look like.

```
const logTitle = (title: string) => {
  console.log(`You clicked ${title}`);
};

const onClick = useCallback(logTitle, [searchTerm]);
```

The useCallback Hook for useEffect

When a function is a dependency for other Hooks, such as `useEffect`, the `useCallback` Hook is needed.

When we pass a function as a dependency to the `useEffect` Hook, we are telling React that the effect should only re-run when the function reference changes.

If we don't memoize the function using `useCallback`, a new function will be created on every component re-render, even if the function's implementation hasn't changed. This means that the effect will re-run unnecessarily, which can cause performance issues in our application.

By wrapping a function in `useCallback`, we ensure that the same function reference is passed as a dependency to `useEffect`. As a result, the effect will only re-run when the function reference changes.

Let's re-visit the previous example. We'll re-use the same `MemoizedBooks` component, but without the `onClick` prop. The `Catalog` component will receive some changes. We'll added the `useEffect` Hook with a function in its dependencies array. This will demonstrate why we need the `useCallback` Hook when functions are dependencies for other Hooks.

```
import { memo, useCallback, useEffect, useState } from 'react';

type Props = {
  searchTerm: string;
};

const Books = ({ searchTerm }: Props) => {
  console.log(`Books list rendered with search term ${searchTerm}.`);
```

```
  // this getBooks() call could be expensive
  const books = getBooks();

  const booksList = books.map(({ title }) => {
    return (
      <li key={title}>{title}</li>
    );
  });

  return (
    <ul>
      {booksList}
    </ul>
  );
}

const MemoizedBooks = memo(Books);

type CatalogProps = {
  searchTerm: string;
};

const Catalog = ({ searchTerm }: CatalogProps) => {
  // Bad: function re-created on every re-render
  const logSearch = () => {
    console.log(`Search term is ${searchTerm}`);
  };

  useEffect(() => {
    logSearch();
  }, [logSearch]);

  return (
    <>
      <MemoizedBooks searchTerm={searchTerm} />
    </>
  );
}

const App = () => {
  const [searchTerm, setSearchTerm] = useState('');
  // used to re-render this component
  const [, setClicks] = useState<number>(0);

  return (
    <>
      <div>
        <input type="text" value={searchTerm} onChange={(event) => setSearchTerm(event.target.value)} />
      </div>
```

```
    <div>
      <button onClick={() => setClicks(clicks => clicks += 1)}>Re-render</b
utton>
    </div>
    <Catalog searchTerm={searchTerm} />
  </>
);
}
```

Clicking the "Re-render" button in the App component logs an extra "Search term is ." message to the console. The same message is already logged once when the component first loads. It shouldn't be logged again when the button is clicked. No search term is included in the logged message because searchTerm is initialized as an empty string.

The problem is that the useEffect Hook re-invokes the logSearch function when the Catalog component re-renders. The useEffect Hook detects that its dependency, the logSearch function, has changed, and re-invokes it. However, the logSearch function doesn't actually change between component re-renders. What changes is its memory reference when its re-created.

We can fix this problem by wrapping the logSearch function with the useCallback Hook.

```
const logSearch = useCallback(() => {
  console.log(`Search term is ${searchTerm}`);
}, [searchTerm]);
```

The searchTerm is added to the useCallback dependencies array. If the searchTerm has not changed, we don't want to re-run the logSearch function. It would just end up logging the same search term to the console. However, if the searchTerm does change, we want to re-run the logSearch function in order to log the new searchTerm to the console.

Now, when we click on the "Re-render" button, no message is logged to the console. The useEffect Hook will only run when logSearch is a new function instance. This will only occur when searchTerm changes from the previous render.

When to use useCallback

As we've seen with the examples above, the useCallback Hook has proved to be a helpful performance optimization. The useCallback Hook memoized the function reference that we provided to it, returning the same function reference between component re-renders - as long as its dependencies didn't change.

The useCallback Hook does not prevent creating a function on every component re-render. The function will still be created on every render. This is expected. What useCallback does is inform React to ignore the newly created function so that it can reference the memoized function instead - as long as its dependencies didn't change.

After seeing the benefit of the useCallback Hook, we might be tempted to use it everywhere. When should we be using the useCallback Hook? To help us answer that question, let's recap the two ideal cases for the useCallback Hook.

- Use useCallback when a function is passed as a prop to a component wrapped in memo. Component re-renders will re-create the function and break the memoization provided by memo.
- Use useCallback when a function is a dependency for other Hooks, like the useEffect Hook. Component re-renders will re-create the function and make useEffect re-run because it thinks that it's dependency changed.

The useCallback Hook should not be used to wrap every function found in React components. There are downsides to doing this.

- It makes the code less readable.
- It ends up degrading performance rather than improving it. Performance degrades because the useCallback Hook is called every time the component re-renders.
- It increases code complexity. The developer must be careful to set the right dependencies for the useCallback Hook and to manage them properly.

If the situation doesn't actually require a performance optimization, the optimization can end up costing more than not having the optimization.

useCallback recap

- Functions in JavaScript are compared by reference, not by value.
- In JavaScript, two identical functions are not equal because they have different references in memory.
- When a React component re-renders, functions defined within that component get re-created and receive new memory references.
- The `useCallback` Hook memoizes a function reference between component re-renders, as long as its dependencies haven't changed.
- The `useCallback` Hook is ideal for functions that are passed as props to components wrapped in `memo`.
- The `useCallback` Hook is also ideal for functions that are dependencies of other Hooks, such as the `useEffect` Hook.
- The `useCallback` Hook is a performance optimization for cases where component re-renders create new function references that trigger more component re-renders.
- Overusing the `useCallback` Hook can actually end up degrading performance rather than optimizing it.

The useTransition Hook

The `useTransition` Hook was introduced in React 18. It was introduced along with the `useDeferredValue` Hook, which we'll also learn about in the next section. These two Hooks make use of React's concurrent rendering to help us build more fluid user experiences in our apps.

Before React 18, rendering was synchronous. Once React started rendering, nothing could stop the rendering until a component was completely rendered. With concurrent rendering in React 18, React can pause the rendering and continue it later, or abort the rendering altogether.

The `useTransition` Hook is used to create *transitions* between different states of the UI. Transitions are a performance improvement. They keep user interface updates responsive, even on slow devices. Transitions allow the UI to remain responsive to the user in the middle of a component re-render. For example, if a user clicks on a tab but then changes their mind, they can click on another tab without waiting for the component re-render caused by their first tab click to finish.

Transitions help distinguish between urgent and non-urgent updates. Urgent updates are expected to respond immediately on the screen, such as when a user types or clicks. Non-urgent updates are those where a slight delay can be acceptable, such as when a list of products are loaded and displayed. The `useTransition` Hook prevents non-urgent updates from blocking the user interface.

Using useTransition

The `useTransition` Hook does not take any parameters. It returns an array with exactly two items.

- An `isPending` flag to tell us if the transition is still pending or not.
- A `startTransition` function that allows us to mark a state update as a transition.

The problem useTransition solves

To better understand the problem that the `useTransition` Hook solves, let's consider the following example. It consists of a very large list of numbers and a search box to search for one number among the list of numbers.

```
import { useState, ChangeEvent, useMemo } from 'react';
```

```
const SearchNumbers = ({ numbers }: { numbers: number[] }) => {
  const [text, setText] = useState("");
  const [query, setQuery] = useState("");

  const handleChange = ({ target: { value } }: ChangeEvent<HTMLInputElement>) => {
    setText(value);
    setQuery(value);
  };

  const numbersList = useMemo(() => (
    numbers.map((i, index) => (
      query
        ? i.toString().startsWith(query)
          && <p key={index}>{i}</p>
        : <p key={index}>{i}</p>
    ))
  ), [query]);

  return (
    <>
      <input onChange={handleChange} value={text} type="text" />

      {numbersList}
    </>
  );
};

const numbers = [...new Array(50000).keys()];

export const App = () => {
  return <SearchNumbers numbers={numbers} />;
};
```

This example uses two states, `setText` and `setQuery`. The `setText` state manages the user's search term that will be used to search through the list of numbers. The `setQuery` state manages the search for results that match the user's search term.

The `handleChange` event handler updates both states, using `setText` to update the search term in the input box and `setQuery` to update the list of matching results.

By default, all updates to state in React are treated as urgent, meaning that they are performed right away. This means that both the `setText` and `setQuery` state updates occur almost simultaneously. React batches both changes and updates them together. This is just React trying to be as efficient as possible, and it works well most of the time. However, when the data that we are dealing with is very large, updating state in batches can be problematic.

The first state update of setText takes very little time, since it just updates the value of the input box. However, the second state update of setQuery takes longer because its query state value is used to filter a large array for matching search results.

React's batching of state updates causes the faster state update (setText) to wait for the slower state update to complete (setQuery). This leads to a situation where there is a considerable amount of delay from when we start typing into the search box until we see our typed characters appear in the search box. Running the example above will demonstrate this.

The useTransition solution

The useTransition Hook allows us to specify any state update as non-urgent. Non-urgent state updates will still occur simultaneously with any other urgent state updates. However, the rendering of the component will not wait for the non-urgent state updates to finish.

Let's fix the example above by including the useTransition Hook. First, let's import the Hook to use it.

```
import { useState, ChangeEvent, useMemo, useTransition } from 'react';
const [isPending, startTransition] = useTransition();
```

Next, let's modify the handleChange event handler, which is where the state updates happen. In this function, we'll mark the state update performed by setResults as non-urgent. We do this by placing it inside the callback function of startTransition.

```
const handleChange = ({ target: { value } }:
ChangeEvent<HTMLInputElement>) => {
  setText(value);
  startTransition(() => {
    setQuery(value);
  });
};
```

Lastly, let's use the boolean isPending variable to show a loading indicator when the startTransition function executes.

```
{isPending ? <div>Loading...</div> : numbersList}
```

Here's the complete code for the example that we fixed with useTransition.

```
import { useState, ChangeEvent, useMemo, useTransition } from 'react';

const SearchNumbers = ({ numbers }: { numbers: number[] }) => {
  const [text, setText] = useState('');
  const [query, setQuery] = useState('');
  const [isPending, startTransition] = useTransition();

  const handleChange = ({ target: { value } }: ChangeEvent<HTMLInputElement>) => {
    setText(value);
    startTransition(() => {
      setQuery(value);
    });
  };

  const numbersList = useMemo(
    () =>
      numbers.map((i, index) =>
        query ? i.toString().startsWith(query) && <p key={index}>{i}</p> : <p key={index}>{i}</p>,
      ),
    [query],
  );

  return (
    <>
      <input onChange={handleChange} value={text} type="text" />

      {isPending ? <div>Loading...</div> : numbersList}
    </>
  );
};

const numbers = [...new Array(50000).keys()];

export const App = () => {
  return <SearchNumbers numbers={numbers} />;
};
```

Fixing a slow tab component

In this next example, there are three tabs, "Home", "Blog", and "Contact". The "Blog" tab renders 500 blog posts using a Post component. The Post component is artificially slowed down to block user interactions with the tabs. When "Blog" is clicked, no other tab can be clicked on until the blog posts are rendered. This is not an ideal user experience.

We should have non-blocking tabs that the user can click on at any time, without having to wait for the content of tabs to be loaded. Let's apply the `useTransition` Hook to create non-blocking transitions for the tabs.

```
import { useState, useTransition, memo, ReactNode } from 'react';

const TabButton = ({
  children,
  isActive,
  onClick,
}: {
  children: ReactNode;
  isActive: boolean;
  onClick: () => void;
}) => {
  if (isActive) {
    return <b>{children}</b>;
  }

  return (
    <button
      onClick={() => {
        onClick();
      }}
    >
      {children}
    </button>
  );
};

const Blog = memo(function BlogTab() {
  const items = [];

  for (let i = 0; i < 500; i++) {
    items.push(<Post key={i} index={i} />);
  }

  return <ul>{items}</ul>;
});

const Post = ({ index }: { index: number }) => {
  let startTime = performance.now();

  while (performance.now() - startTime < 1) {
```

```
    // Add a 1ms delay to simulate slow code
  }

  return <li>Post {index + 1}</li>;
};

const TabContainer = () => {
  const [isPending, startTransition] = useTransition();
  const [tab, setTab] = useState('home');

  const selectTab = (nextTab: string) => {
    startTransition(() => {
      setTab(nextTab);
    });
  };

  return (
    <>
      <TabButton isActive={tab === 'home'} onClick={() => selectTab('home')}>
        Home
      </TabButton>
      <TabButton isActive={tab === 'blog'} onClick={() => selectTab('blog')}>
        Blog
      </TabButton>
      <TabButton
        isActive={tab === 'contact'}
        onClick={() => selectTab('contact')}
      >
        Contact
      </TabButton>
      <hr />
      {isPending && <p>Loading...</p>}
      {!isPending && (
        <>
          {tab === 'home' && <h1>Home</h1>}
          {tab === 'blog' && <Blog />}
          {tab === 'contact' && <h1>Contact</h1>}
        </>
      )}
    </>
  );
};

export const App = () => <TabContainer />;
```

We marked the `setTab` state update, performed in the `selectTab` function, as non-urgent by placing it inside the callback function of `startTransition`.

Now, when we click on the "Blog" tab and then immediately click on the "Contact" tab, it interrupts the slow render of the "Blog" tab. The "Contact" tab shows right away. Marking the state update as a transition prevented slow re-renders from freezing the user interface.

We used the `isPending` boolean value returned by `useTransition` to indicate to the user that a transition is in progress. We displayed a "Loading..." message during the transition. Transitions between the "Home" and "Contact" tabs are very quick, so the loading message is hardly seen. The loading message can be seen after clicking on the "Blog" tab - until the content of the tab has loaded.

The `Blog` component is a memorized version of the `BlogTab` component. We use the memoized `Blog` component in the `TabContainer` component so that React does not re-render `BlogTab` every time the `TabContainer` re-renders. This prevent useless re-renders of the `BlogTab` component. The `BlogTab` component does not need to be re-rendered frequently since it renders the same data every time.

useTransition recap

- The `useTransition` Hook helps you keep your UI responsive to users, even when dealing with large amounts of data.
- Transitions created with the `useTransition` Hook keep user interface updates responsive, even on slow devices.
- Mark state updates as non-blocking transitions with `startTransition`.
- Notify users with a loading indicator when a transition is pending - when `isPending` is `true`.
- Don't use the `useTransition` Hook everywhere. Use it only if you have a complex component that can't be optimized by any other means.

The useDeferredValue Hook

The `useDeferredValue` Hook was introduced in React 18. This Hook accepts a value and returns a new copy of the value that will defer to more urgent updates. It can help you improve the performance and user experience of your React app by deferring the update of some part of the user interface.

Using useDeferredValue

The `useDeferredValue` Hook takes one parameter, the value to defer. This value can be of any type. Call the `useDeferredValue` Hook at the top level of a component to get a deferred version of a value.

```
import { useState, useDeferredValue } from 'react';

const SearchPage = () => {
  const [query, setQuery] = useState('');
  const deferredQuery = useDeferredValue(query);
  // ...
}
```

During the initial render of the component, the deferred value will be the same as the initial value provided. In the example above, `deferredQuery` will be the same as `query`.

During component re-renders, the deferred value will be updated, but with a delay. The deferred value will *lag behind* the latest value. This delay allows React to prioritize other updates that are more important for the user experience, such as typing or scrolling.

useTransition versus useDeferredValue

The `useTransition` Hook gives us full control, allowing us to decide what code should be treated as non-urgent, or low-priority.

However, we don't always have access to the non-urgent state updating code in order to wrap it with the `startTransition` function provided by the `useTransition` Hook. This could because the state update is performed by a third-party library, or because the state update is performed by a component that we have no control over. In such cases, we can use the useDeferredValue Hook instead.

With useDeferredValue, we don't wrap the state updating code. We only wrap the value that's changed because of the state update.

We shouldn't use both useTransition and useDeferredValue Hooks together, since they achieve the same goal.

Let's look at an example where useDeferredValue is used to wrap the value for a user's search query.

```
import { useState, useMemo, useDeferredValue, ChangeEvent } from "react";

const numbers = [...new Array(150000).keys()];

const SearchList = () => {
  const [query, setQuery] = useState("");

  const handleChange = (e: ChangeEvent<HTMLInputElement>) => {
    setQuery(e.target.value);
  };

  return (
    <div>
      <input type="number" onChange={handleChange} value={query} />
      <List query={query} />
    </div>
  );
};

const List = ({ query }: { query: string }) => {
  const deferredQuery = useDeferredValue(query);

  const list = useMemo(() => (
    numbers.map((i, index) => (
      deferredQuery
        ? i.toString().startsWith(deferredQuery)
          && <p key={index}>{i}</p>
        : <p key={index}>{i}</p>
    ))
  ), [deferredQuery]);

  return (
    <div>
```

```
      {list}
    </div>
  );
}

export { SearchList };
```

The state for query in the `SearchList` component will update immediately, so that the input will display the new value typed by the user. The search query is then passed along as a prop to the `List` component, where search results are displayed.

The `SearchList` component is the parent component. Let's assume that we have no control over the parent component. Therefore, we can't use the `useTransition` Hook here because we don't have access to the state updating code.

Instead, we can use the `useDeferredValue` Hook to tell React that the query prop passed to the `List` component will trigger a transition update. We pass the query prop value to the `useDeferredValue` Hook and use the deferred value that is returned in the `List` component. React will defer the expensive rendering of the search results to allow the more urgent update to the search input to take place first.

The deferredQuery variable will keep its previous value until new data has been loaded. If we enter a "1" in the search input, wait for the results to load, and then edit the search query to be "12", we'll see stale search results until the new search results have loaded. React will re-render with the new query ("12") but with the old deferredQuery ("1"). The deferredQuery value *lags behind* the query value.

The deferring done by `useDeferredValue` is interruptible. If we type into the search input a second time, React will abandon the deferral of the first value and restart with the deferral of the new value. The latest provided value will always be used.

We can really see the difference that `useDeferredValue` makes when we enter the first number to search by ("1"). This is because iterating over 150,000 numbers in the `List` component is very expensive. It ends up blocking updates to search input when `useDeferredValue` is not used. Try running the example above with and without `useDeferredValue` to see the difference.

useDeferredValue recap

- `useDeferredValue` allows React to perform other state or UI updates with a higher priority than updates related to the value that it wraps.
- `useDeferredValue` is not *debouncing* or *throttling*. Debouncing is waiting for the user to stop typing before updating the list. Throttling is updating the list within a specified time interval.
- `useDeferredValue` is better suited than *debouncing* or *throttling* to optimizing rendering because it's built into React.
- `useDeferredValue` doesn't require choosing a fixed amount of delay like *debouncing* or *throttling* does.
- Don't use the `useDeferredValue` Hook everywhere. Use it only if you have a complex component that can't be optimized by any other means.

Profiling

The best way to use memo, useMemo, and useCallback is in response to a performance issue. The memoization provided by memo, useMemo and useCallback can help speed up slow component renders. If we notice that our app has become sluggish, we can profile our app to track down the components that are taking longer to render.

Profiler tab

The **React Developer Tools** (https://react.dev/learn/react-developer-tools) browser extension adds a new Profiler tab to the browser's DevTools with an interactive profiler.

The Profiler tab provides a visual representation of the rendering performance of our application by showing a hierarchy of components and their rendering times.

The Profiler tab helps with identifying components that are causing performance issues. By analyzing the rendering times of each component, we can identify the components that take longer to render than others. Then, we can use the memoization provided by memo, useMemo and useCallback to optimize these components, improving the overall performance of our React application.

React Profiler

React provides a built-in profiling tool called the React Profiler that we can use to measure and analyze the performance of our React application. The React Profiler helps us identify components that are causing performance issues. These components will benefit from optimizations such as memoization.

Profiling adds some additional overhead to the React application, so it is disabled in production. We can only profile a React application in development mode.

React provides a Profiler component that allow us to measure the rendering performance of a component or a component tree. It's a lightweight component, but it should be used only when necessary. Keep in mind that each usage of the Profiler component adds some CPU and memory overhead to the application.

The Profiler component can be added anywhere in a React tree to measure the cost of rendering that part of the tree. It requires two props: an id and an onRender callback function. The onRender callback function will be called by React whenever a component within the tree commits an update.

> *Committing an update means that React has finished rendering the changes made to the virtual DOM and has applied those changes to the actual DOM.*

Multiple `Profiler` components can be used in the same component to measure different parts of the component tree.

```
import { Profiler, useState } from 'react';

const Sidebar = () => {
  const [count, setCount] = useState(0);

  return (
    <>
      <p>Sidebar</p>
      <button onClick={() => setCount(count + 1)}>{count}</button>
    </>
  );
};

const Content = () => {
  const [count, setCount] = useState(0);

  return (
    <>
      <p>Content</p>
      <button onClick={() => setCount(count + 1)}>{count}</button>
    </>
  );
};

const App = () => {
  const onRender = (
    id: string,
    phase: 'mount' | 'update' | 'nested-update',
    actualDuration: number,
    baseDuration: number,
    startTime: number,
    commitTime: number,
  ) => {
    console.log(`${id}'s ${phase} phase:`);
    console.log(`Actual duration: ${actualDuration}`);
```

```
    console.log(`Base duration: ${baseDuration}`);
    console.log(`Start time: ${startTime}`);
    console.log(`Commit time: ${commitTime}`);
  };

  return (
    <>
      <Profiler id="Sidebar" onRender={onRender}>
        <Sidebar />
      </Profiler>
      <Profiler id="Content" onRender={onRender}>
        <Content />
      </Profiler>
    </>
  );
};

export { App };
```

The onRender method that we defined in the App component logs the data provided to us by the Profiler component. Let's go over each parameter returned by the onRender callback function of the Profiler component.

- **id**: The string id prop of the Profiler that we set.
- **phase**: Informs us if the component tree has just been mounted for the first time or if it re-rendered due to a change in props, state, or Hooks.
- **actualDuration**: The number of milliseconds spent rendering the component tree. If we applied memoization using memo, useMemo, and useCallback, this number will reveal if the memoization is actually optimizing the component tree or not. When comparing the actualDuration of a component's initial mount with the actualDuration of component updates, we should expect updates to show a decrease in the actualDuration. This is the result of preventing unnecessary component re-renders. If there is no such decrease and memoization strategies were applied, then the memoization is not working as expected.
- **baseDuration**: The number of milliseconds estimating how much time it would take to re-render the entire component tree without any optimizations. It's calculated by adding up the durations of the most recent render for each component in the tree. This value estimates a worst-case cost of rendering. It can be compared against actualDuration to see if memoization is actually working or not.
- **startTime**: A numeric timestamp representing when React began rendering the current update.

- **endTime**: A numeric timestamp representing when committed the current update.

Nesting the React Profiler

Profiler components can also be nested within each other. Nesting the `Profiler` component is useful when we want to measure the performance of specific child components in more detail.

Let's nest a new `Profiler` within the `Profiler` that is used for the `Content` component. We'll use this new `Profiler` to measure specific performance details for an `Editor` component.

```
import { Profiler, ReactNode, useState } from "react";

const Sidebar = () => {
  return (
    <p>Sidebar</p>
  );
};

type ContentProps = {
  children: ReactNode;
};

const Content = ({ children }: ContentProps) => {
  const [count, setCount] = useState(0);

  return (
    <>
      <p>Content</p>
      <button onClick={() => setCount(count + 1)}>{count}</button>
      <div>{children}</div>
    </>
  );
};

const Editor = () => {
  const [count, setCount] = useState(0);

  return (
    <>
      <p>Editor</p>
      <button onClick={() => setCount(count + 1)}>{count}</button>
    </>
  );
};

const Preview = () => {
```

```
  const [count, setCount] = useState(0);

  return (
    <>
      <p>Preview</p>
      <button onClick={() => setCount(count + 1)}>{count}</button>
    </>
  );
};

const App = () => {
  const onRender = (
    id: string,
    phase: 'mount' | 'update' | 'nested-update',
    actualDuration: number,
    baseDuration: number,
    startTime: number,
    commitTime: number,
  ) => {
    console.log(`${id}'s ${phase} phase:`);
    console.log(`Actual duration: ${actualDuration}`);
    console.log(`Base duration: ${baseDuration}`);
    console.log(`Start time: ${startTime}`);
    console.log(`Commit time: ${commitTime}`);
  };

  return (
    <>
      <Profiler id="Sidebar" onRender={onRender}>
        <Sidebar />
      </Profiler>
      <Profiler id="Content" onRender={onRender}>
        <Content>
          <Profiler id="Editor" onRender={onRender}>
            <Editor />
          </Profiler>
          <Preview />
        </Content>
      </Profiler>
    </>
  );
};

export { App };
```

Profiling a slow component

The above profiling examples were very basic in order to demonstrate how the `Profiler` component can be used. We didn't really encounter any performance bottlenecks there.

In the following example, we'll look at a more realistic scenario where the `Profiler` component is used to profile a component that turns out to have performance issues.

```
import { Profiler, useEffect, useState } from 'react';

// This component takes a long time to render
const SlowComponent = () => {
  const [data, setData] = useState<number[]>([]);

  // Simulate a long-running operation
  useEffect(() => {
    const timeout = setTimeout(() => {
      setData([1, 2, 3, 4, 5]);
    }, 5000);

    return () => {
      clearTimeout(timeout);
    };
  }, []);

  return (
    <div>
      {data.map((item) => (
        <div key={item}>{item}</div>
      ))}
    </div>
  );
};

const App = () => {
  const [showSlowComponent, setShowSlowComponent] = useState(false);

  const onRender = (
    id: string,
    phase: 'mount' | 'update' | 'nested-update',
    actualDuration: number,
    baseDuration: number,
    startTime: number,
    commitTime: number,
  ) => {
    if (id === 'SlowComponent') {
      console.log(`${id}'s ${phase} phase:`);
      console.log(`Actual duration: ${actualDuration}`);
      console.log(`Base duration: ${baseDuration}`);
      console.log(`Start time: ${startTime}`);
      console.log(`Commit time: ${commitTime}`);
    }
  };
```

```
  return (
    <Profiler id="App" onRender={onRender}>
      <button onClick={() => setShowSlowComponent(!showSlowComponent)}>
        {showSlowComponent ? 'Hide' : 'Show'} Slow Component
      </button>
      {showSlowComponent && (
        <Profiler id="SlowComponent" onRender={onRender}>
          <SlowComponent />
        </Profiler>
      )}
    </Profiler>
  );
};

export { App };
```

We used the JavaScript `setTimeout` function in the `useEffect` Hook of `SlowComponent` to simulate a slow API call when the component mounts. This will introduce a five second delay from the time the component mounts to the time the component is updated to display its data.

When `SlowComponent` mounts, the `onRender` function will log the following to the console.

```
SlowComponent's mount phase:
Actual duration: 0.10000002384185791
Base duration: 0.10000002384185791
Start time: 193841.39999997616
Commit time: 193841.70000004768
```

When `SlowComponent` updates, the `onRender` function will log the following to the console.

```
SlowComponent's update phase:
Actual duration: 1.2999999523162842
Base duration: 1.100000023841858
Start time: 196853.80000007153
Commit time: 196855.20000004768
```

The `actualDuration` increased for the component update phase. When the `actualDuration` increases during the component update phase, it means that the component is taking longer to render for subsequent updates. This could be an indication of a performance issue in the component. The component might be doing more work than necessary on each update, or it might be re-rendering unnecessarily.

In this case, the performance issue is the slow API call that we simulated. If it was a real API call, the cause of the performance issue could be a server-side issue with the API, or we might be requesting too much data from it all at once.

Profiling improvement

Let's use the React `Profiler` to compare the renders of a non-memoized component versus a memoized component. This will demonstrate how we can use the `Profiler` to make performance improvements to our React application on a component-by-component basis.

In the following example, a `Todos` component is used to display a list of to-do items. An App component will render both the non-memoized `Todos` component and the `MemoizedTodos` component - which has been memoized with `memo`. We'll wrap each of these components in a `Profiler` to compare their `actualDuration` values.

```
import { memo, useState, Profiler } from 'react';

type Item = {
  id: number;
  title: string;
};

type TodosProps = {
  list: Item[];
};

const Todos = ({ list }: TodosProps) => {
  return (
    <ul>
      {list.map((item) => (
        <li key={item.id}>{item.title}</li>
      ))}
    </ul>
  );
};

const MemoizedTodos = memo(Todos);

const App = () => {
  const [todo, setTodo] = useState([
    { id: 1, title: 'Read book' },
    { id: 2, title: 'Clean room' },
    { id: 3, title: 'Make coffee' },
  ]);
  const [todoText, setTodoText] = useState('');

  const addTodo = () => {
    const id = Math.max(...todo.map((p) => p.id), 0) + 1;
    const newTodo = { id, title: todoText };
    setTodo([...todo, newTodo]);
```

```
  };

  const onRender = (
    id: string,
    phase: 'mount' | 'update' | 'nested-update',
    actualDuration: number,
    baseDuration: number,
    startTime: number,
    commitTime: number
  ) => {
    console.log(`${id}'s ${phase} phase:`);
    console.log(`Actual duration: ${actualDuration}`);
    console.log(`Base duration: ${baseDuration}`);
    console.log(`Start time: ${startTime}`);
    console.log(`Commit time: ${commitTime}`);
  };

  return (
    <div>
      <input
        type="text"
        value={todoText}
        onChange={(e) => setTodoText(e.target.value)}
      />
      <button type="button" onClick={addTodo}>
        Add Todo
      </button>

      <Profiler id="Todos" onRender={onRender}>
        <Todos list={todo} />
      </Profiler>

      <Profiler id="MemoizedTodos" onRender={onRender}>
        <MemoizedTodos list={todo} />
      </Profiler>
    </div>
  );
};

export { App };
```

The App component will re-render every time we make a change to the text input. Let's add a character in the text input and see what the `onRender` function will log to the console.

```
Todos's update phase:
Actual duration: 0.10000038146972656
Base duration: 0
Start time: 7810.599999427795
Commit time: 7810.800000190735
```

```
MemoizedTodos's update phase:
Actual duration: 0
Base duration: 0.09999942779541016
Start time: 7810.699999809265
Commit time: 7810.800000190735
```

Notice that the `actualDuration` for the update of `MemoizedTodos` is zero, while the `actualDuration` for the update of `Todos` is just slightly greater than zero.

Using `memo` on the `Todos` component has given us a slight performance gain. When the list of to-do items does not change, the `MemoizedTodos` component is not re-rendered. Re-rendering the component for each character typed in the text input is wasteful in terms of performance. `memo` helped us prevent unnecessary component re-renders. It's the reason why the `actualDuration` of `MemoizedTodos` is zero.

Profiling recap

- Profiling is the process of measuring the performance of a React application, which involves identifying and resolving performance issues.
- Profiling can help developers understand which components are causing performance bottlenecks.
- The Google Chrome React Developer Tools extension provides a Profiler tab that generates a visual representation of the rendering performance of components.
- The React `Profiler` component is a built-in tool that can be used for profiling and optimizing React components and applications.
- Profiling can help us optimize our React applications for better performance and a smoother user experience.

Styling React components

React doesn't have a strong opinion about how we define and use CSS to style our components. In this section, we'll look at the following component styling strategies.

- Inline styling.
- Styling via CSS files.
- CSS modules.
- Sass & SCSS.

Inline styling

Inline styling in React is similar to how HTML tags can be styled with the `style` attribute.

We can add inline styles to any React element. Let's look at an example.

```
const Heading = () => {
  return (
    <div style={{ border: '1px solid #333', padding: '2rem' }}>
      <h1
        style={{
          fontSize: '2rem',
          padding: '1rem',
          backgroundColor: 'green',
          color: 'white',
        }}
      >
        Main Heading
      </h1>
      <p>Main description</p>
    </div>
  );
};

export { Heading };
```

Notice that the `style` attribute has two sets of curly brackets. The first set of curly brackets for the `style` attribute injects JavaScript into the JSX. The second, or inner set of curly brackets, creates a JavaScript object with CSS rules. This object contains *camelCase* CSS properties that will be applied to the element. Since this is a JavaScript object, we write its attributes in camelCase. Each CSS property is separated by a comma.

245

The camelCase object properties will be converted to standard CSS attributes during compilation. For example, `backgroundColor` will become `background-color`. It's only the CSS property names that are converted from camelCase to dash-separated names. CSS property values are not converted.

We can also assign CSS style objects to variables. Using TypeScript, these style objects receive the `CSSProperties` type. We can then assign this object to the `style` attribute of the element that needs to be styled. Let's take a look at an example of this.

```
import { CSSProperties } from 'react';

const Greeting = () => {
  const Container: CSSProperties = {
    border: '1px solid #ccc',
    padding: '2rem',
  };

  const Title: CSSProperties = {
    fontSize: '1.5rem',
    padding: '1rem',
    backgroundColor: '#ccc',
    color: '#333',
  };

  return (
    <div style={Container}>
      <h1 style={Title}>Welcome!</h1>
      <p>Welcome to the site.</p>
    </div>
  );
};

export { Greeting };
```

Inline styling is helpful for quickly prototyping what we want our user interface to look like. However, it does not scale very well.

Using the `style` attribute to style elements may not seem all that bad when we only have a few CSS properties to add. However, what if we have several CSS properties to add? This is where inline styling starts to get out of hand.

In React applications, we usually need to reuse styles across multiple components. Inline styling isn't great for this. As a result, using inline styling is not recommended for large projects.

CSS file

Using a CSS file to style components involves writing CSS selectors and rules in a separate CSS file. The CSS file can then be imported and applied to one or many components. It's similar to linking a CSS file in a HTML file via the `<head>` tag.

We simply need to create a new CSS file in our project, add CSS selectors and rules within it, and then import it into one or many React component files. The CSS file import goes at the top of a React file, where all other imports are placed.

Component-specific CSS file

Let's take a look at an example of a `Product` component in a `Product.tsx` file that imports a `Product.css` file.

```
import './Product.css';

type Props = {
  name: string;
  price: number;
};

const Product = ({ name, price }: Props) => {
  return (
    <div className="Product">
      <h1 className="ProductName">{name}</h1>
      <p className="ProductPrice">{price}</p>
    </div>
  );
};

export { Product };
```

In the `Product.css` file, we must add CSS selectors for the CSS classes that we used in the `Product` component via `className`. Then, we can add CSS rules for these CSS selectors.

```
.Product {
  border: 1px solid black;
  padding: 1rem;
}

.ProductName {
  font-weight: bold;
  background: black;
```

```css
  color: white;
  padding: 1rem;
}

.ProductPrice {
  font-style: italic;
}
```

We have the option to use the `Product.css` file only for the `Product` component. Or, we can reuse `Product.css` for other components that need to make use of its product-related CSS selectors and rules.

However, since the `Product.css` file has very specific CSS selectors and rules that are tightly coupled with the `Product` component, we probably shouldn't reuse it in other components. This will help us avoid running into clashing class names.

Clashing class names happens when two or more CSS classes have the same name, and the styling rules defined in each of them conflict with each other.

Global CSS file

We can create a global CSS file that will be used across all pages of our React application. To do so, we must import this CSS file in the main file of our application. In a React application created with Vite, this would be the `main.tsx` file.

Creating a React app with Vite automatically adds an `index.css` file import in `main.tsx` for us.

```
import React from 'react'
import ReactDOM from 'react-dom/client'
import App from './App'
import './index.css'

ReactDOM.createRoot(document.getElementById('root') as HTMLElement).render(
  <React.StrictMode>
    <App />
  </React.StrictMode>,
)
```

We can remove the default styles that are included in the `index.css` file by Vite's project scaffolding. Then, we can add the global styles that we need for our project.

Here are some examples of global styles that we might want to set for our project.

```css
a {
  font-weight: bold;
  color: #333;
}

a:hover,
a:active,
a:focus {
  color: #000;
}

body {
  margin: 0;
  padding: 0;
}

h1 {
  font-size: 4rem;
  font-weight: bold;
  margin: 0 0 2rem;
}
```

Using CSS files is a more effective solution compared to using inline styles. CSS selectors and rules are isolated to their own specific file rather than being embedded in React files. This keeps the codebase more organized.

Another benefit of using CSS files is reusability. A CSS file can be used globally across the entire app, or reused across multiple components.

CSS files can become problematic when working on large projects. We can run into situations where the class names defined in one CSS file end up clashing with class names defined in other CSS files. The results can end up being unpredictable.

CSS Modules

CSS Modules allow us to use the same class name in multiple files without naming clashes. This is because each class name is given a unique programmatic name. This is helpful when developing larger applications. Every class name that we define in a CSS Module is scoped locally to the specific component that imports it.

A CSS Module stylesheet is similar to a regular CSS stylesheet. The only difference is that it has a different file extension of `.module.css`.

Let's create a `Success` component that makes use of a CSS Module, `Success.module.css`.

```
import styles from './Success.module.css';

type SuccessSize = 'Small' | 'Large';

type Props = {
  message: string;
  size?: SuccessSize;
};

const Success = ({ message, size }: Props) => {
  const classNames = size ? `${styles.Success} ${styles[size]}` : styles.Success;

  return <p className={classNames}>{message}</p>;
};

export { Success };
```

The `Success` component receives a `message` to display and an optional `size` prop that configures the font size of the success message. We can use component props to assign classes from a CSS Module.

If the `size` prop is defined, then the paragraph element will receive two classes, the `Success` class and a class for the specified `size`. If the `size` prop is not defined, then the paragraph element will only receive a `Success` class.

Using `styles.Success` references a `.Success` class from the imported CSS Module. Using `styles[size]` references either a `.Small` or a `.Large` class from the imported CSS Module, depending on what the value for `size` is.

Now, let's create the CSS Module for the `Success` component and name it `Success.module.css`. Let's add some styles to the CSS classes that we used in the `Success` component.

```
.Success {
  padding: 1rem;
  background-color: green;
  color: white;
  border-radius: 1rem;
  margin: 0 0 2rem;
}

.Success.Small {
  font-size: 10px;
}

.Success.Large {
  font-size: 20px;
}
```

Importing and using a CSS Module automatically scopes the styles that we defined using the format [filename]_[classname]_[hash]. In the browser, if we inspect the success message displayed on the screen, the final result will look something like this.

```
<p class="Success_Success_sdfg431">Some message...</p>
```

As we've seen in this example, dynamically assigning classes and styling via component props is quick and easy with CSS Modules.

You may have noticed that some class names in the CSS Module are stuck together in a single CSS rule, such as Success.Small, for example. This is because both the Success and Small classes can be used on the same paragraph element in the Success component. Using .Success.Small allows us to target a paragraph element that contains both classes.

Sass & SCSS

Sass is an extension language for CSS and is commonly referred to as a CSS preprocessor. It adds special features to CSS, such as variables, nested selectors and rules, and mixins. It's basically CSS with superpowers!

Sass supports two different syntaxes. The most popular is the SCSS syntax. It uses the file extension .scss. SCSS is a superset of CSS, which means that all valid CSS is also valid SCSS. SCSS syntax is very similar to CSS, making it the easiest Sass syntax to learn and use.

Vite provides built-in support for `.scss` files. There is no need to install Vite-specific plugins for SCSS files. The only thing that must be installed is the Sass pre-processor itself. Here's how to install the Sass pre-processor.

```
# use npm to install support for .scss and .sass
npm install -D sass

# or, use yarn to install support for .scss and .sass
yarn add -D sass
```

CSS Modules can also be used in combination with Sass by prepending `.module` to the `.scss` file extension, resulting in a file extension of `.module.scss`.

Let's update the `Success` component so that it makes use of a Sass Module. To do so, we'll change the CSS Module import to a Sass Module import.

```
import styles from './Success.module.scss';
```

Now, let's add styles to this Sass Module for the `Success` component.

```scss
$text-color: green;
$border-color: black;

.Success {
  padding: 1rem;
  border: 1px solid $border-color;
  color: $text-color;

  &.Small {
    font-size: 10px;
  }

  &.Large {
    font-size: 20px;
  }
}
```

Sass allows us to define variables like `$text-color` and `$border-color`. Sass also allows us to nest CSS selectors so that we can organize the `Small` and `Large` classes neatly within the `Success` class. This makes it easier to read the styles defined in the file.

To learn more about what's possible with Sass, consult the Sass documentation (https://sass-lang.com/documentation).

Recap

- Inline styling can come in handy when prototyping a React component, but it is not recommended for large projects.
- Using CSS files is more practical than inline styling, but there is risk that duplicate class names can end up clashing.
- CSS Modules are a convenient solution for styling React components without any risk of naming clashes across larger projects.
- CSS Modules use the `.module.css` file extension.
- Sass can be used to give CSS superpowers. Sass can be used with CSS Modules by using the `.module.scss` file extension.

Context

React context allows a component to receive information from its distant parents without having to receive it directly via props.

Passing props down into a deeply nested component hierarchy, until we reach our destination component, creates a problem known as *prop drilling*. React context is the ideal way to ease the pain of prop drilling.

Why React context?

Passing data to React components is usually handled via component props. For example, we use props to pass data from a parent component to a child component.

However, passing props can quickly get out of hand if there are several components sitting in between our parent component and the destination child component. Also, if many components in our application need access to the same data, we'll end up having to pass the same props everywhere. Our application will quickly become messy and unmaintainable.

React context aims to solve the problems that come with *prop drilling*. Prop drilling is when data needs to pass as props across several nested child components in order to get to the destination component.

The "drilling" relates to the fact that several nested child components are forced to receive props that they do not actually need. They just receive these props in order to pass them down to more deeply-nested components that might need them.

Prop drilling can affect the reusability of components, making them more difficult to re-use. Prop drilling also makes components more difficult to test.

Context allows a parent component to make its data available to components in the component tree below it. It doesn't matter how deep in the component tree a child component is, it will be able to access that data without having to receive it as props.

Before using context

We shouldn't always use React context every time we need to pass some props a few levels deep. Before using context, we should consider if using props, or using the special `children` prop, are sufficient for our needs.

Sharing state between React components is a common challenge. The first solution we should consider for sharing state is to lift state up to the closest common parent component. Lifting state may result in prop drilling. If the prop drilling becomes complex, then we should consider using context.

Whenever we find ourselves passing props to visual components that don't directly need them, we should consider using the `children` prop before considering context.

Consider the following example where we are passing a `posts` prop to a `Layout` component that, internally, forwards the `posts` prop to a `Posts` component.

```
<Layout posts={posts} />
```

Instead, we can have the `Layout` component receive a `children` prop rather than a `posts` prop.

```
<Layout><Posts posts={posts} /></Layout>
```

Passing a `posts` prop to the `Layout` component, only to have it forwarded to the `Posts` component, seems unnecessary. Instead, we can assign the `posts` prop directly to the component that needs it, the `Posts` component, and use the `children` prop to get `Posts` component into the `Layout` component. This reduces the amount of layers between the component that provides the data and the component that actually uses it.

Using context wisely

React context is not a state management system like **Redux** (https://redux.js.org). Therefore, we must be careful to use context wisely.

React context is meant for data that does not need to be updated often. It works best for data that you can write once, read any number of times, and update very rarely, or never at all.

Context does not work well for data that needs to be updated frequently. This is because when a value of a context provider changes, the components that make use of that context will re-render, even if they don't use the value that changed.

A common approach is to to set React context at the application level, that is, at the top-most level of an application. This is done in order to share data across the entire application. Storing data at this level is similar to using global variables, but without the problems associated with global variables.

Here are some examples of data that usually gets stored in React context at the application level.

- Theme data (light mode, dark mode)
- User data (for the logged-in user)
- Location-specific data (location, language, currency)

We can set up many different contexts across our app and have them exist in parallel. We can have an application-level context for application settings. We can also have more localized context for a parent component that provides data to the component tree below it.

Using context

The React `useContext` Hook allows us to read from a context. Just like with other React Hooks, we must make sure to call `useContext` at the top of our component.

```
import { useContext } from 'react';

const App = () => {
  const theme = useContext(ThemeContext);

  // ...
};

export { App };
```

The `useContext` Hook returns the *context value* for the context that we passed to it, which is `ThemeContext` here. To get the context value, React will search the component tree and find the closest *context provider* for that particular context.

`ThemeContext` refers to a context that will need to have already been created with the `createContext` function.

Let's take a look at an example of how to create a context using the `createContext` function. We'll then use a context provider in an App component to make that context available for all of App's sub-components.

```
import { createContext, useContext, ReactNode } from 'react';

const ThemeContext = createContext<string | undefined>(undefined);

type PanelProps = {
  title: string;
  children: ReactNode;
};

const Panel = ({ title, children }: PanelProps) => {
  const theme = useContext(ThemeContext);

  return (
    <section className={`panel-${theme}`}>
      <h5>{title}</h5>
      {children}
      <p>Theme: {theme}</p>
    </section>
  );
};

const Form = () => {
  return (
    <div>
      <Panel title="Welcome, User">
        <button>Sign up</button>
        <button>Log in</button>
      </Panel>
    </div>
  );
};

const App = () => {
  return (
    <ThemeContext.Provider value="dark">
      <Form />
    </ThemeContext.Provider>
  );
};

export { App };
```

We created a theme-related context and stored it in a `ThemeContext` variable. We gave this context a default value of `undefined`.

When React can't find any context providers for a particular context in the parent's component tree, the value returned by `useContext` will be equal to the default value that was specified when creating the context - which was `undefined`. Since we defined a context provider for the `ThemeContext` in the App component, the default value of `undefined` will never be returned.

We also have the option to use a more meaningful default value for context instead of `undefined`. In this case, we could have used a string representing the default theme name. Here's what that would look like.

```
const ThemeContext = createContext<string>('dark');
```

After having created the `ThemeContext`, we used a `ThemeContext.Provider` with a value of `"dark"` to let the sub-component tree of the App component know that the current theme is the `"dark"` theme.

If we forget to specify a `value` for the context provider, it's like passing undefined. A context value of undefined would be passed to all sub-components that reference that context.

The `Panel` component above reads the `ThemeContext` via the `useContext` Hook and retrieves the current theme value, which is `"dark"`.

No matter how many levels of components there are between the context provider and the `Panel` component, when the `Panel` calls `useContext(ThemeContext)`, it will receive `"dark"` as the context value.

The `ThemeContext` itself does not hold the theme information of `"dark"`. The `ThemeContext` is just a representation for any theme-related information that we want to make available to components.

For now, the theme that we get back from the `ThemeContext` will always be dark mode. There are times when we need context to change. We can update context by combining it with state.

Let's declare a state variable for `theme` in the App component. Then, let's pass the current state as the context value for the context provider. This will allow the `Panel` component to get the most recently selected theme via the `useContext` Hook.

```
import { createContext, useContext, ReactNode, useState } from 'react';

const ThemeContext = createContext<string>("dark");

// ...

const App = () => {
  const [theme, setTheme] = useState<string>("dark");

  const changeTheme = () => {
    setTheme(theme => theme === 'light' ? 'dark' : 'light');
  };

  return (
    <ThemeContext.Provider value={theme}>
      <button onClick={changeTheme}>
        Change Theme
      </button>
      <hr />
      <Form />
    </ThemeContext.Provider>
  );
};

export { App };
```

We introduced a "Change Theme" button in the App component. When clicked, the changeTheme callback function is called, invoking the setTheme state setter function that toggles the theme.

When we click on the "Change Theme" button, we will see the name of the currently active theme displayed within the Panel component.

Overriding context

We can override context for a specific section of the component tree. To do so, we just need to wrap a specific section of the component tree with a context provider that has a different value set.

Let's take a look at an example of how to override context. The App component below will use a theme context provider with a value of "dark". The Form component, used by the App component, will then override the theme context for the Footer component that it makes use of.

```
import { createContext, useContext, ReactNode } from 'react';
```

259

```
const ThemeContext = createContext<string>('dark');

type PanelProps = {
  title: string;
  children: ReactNode;
};

const Panel = ({ title, children }: PanelProps) => {
  const theme = useContext(ThemeContext);

  return (
    <section className={`panel-${theme}`}>
      <h5>{title}</h5>
      <p>Panel Theme: {theme}</p>
      {children}
    </section>
  );
};

const Footer = () => {
  const theme = useContext(ThemeContext);

  return (
    <footer>
      <p>&copy; React App</p>
      <p>Footer Theme: {theme}</p>
    </footer>
  );
};

const Form = () => {
  return (
    <Panel title="Welcome, User">
      <button>Sign up</button>
      <button>Log in</button>
      <hr />
      <ThemeContext.Provider value="light">
        <Footer />
      </ThemeContext.Provider>
    </Panel>
  );
};

const App = () => {
  return (
    <ThemeContext.Provider value="dark">
      <Form />
    </ThemeContext.Provider>
  );
};
```

```
export { App };
```

In the App component above, the Form component is wrapped with a ThemeContext provider with a value of "dark". However, in the Form component, the Footer component is wrapped with a ThemeContext provider with a value of "light".

The Panel component receives a value of "dark" from the useContext Hook. However, the Footer component receives a value of "light" from the useContext Hook.

We have successfully overridden the context for a specific section of the component tree, which was the Footer component in this example.

Using multiple contexts

We can use multiple independent contexts in our React application. The example below uses two separate contexts. ThemeContext manages the current theme, which is represented as a string. UserContext manages the current user, which is represented as an object. This object contains the user's name and an updater function to update the user's name.

It's usually a good idea to have separate contexts. A good strategy is to separate contexts by responsibility. By doing so, we can avoid creating one large context for the entire React application.

Having one large context for the entire application will cause the whole app to re-render whenever any context value is updated. Separating contexts help us avoid creating this type of performance bottleneck for our application.

Let's take a look at how we can use both ThemeContext and UserContext in an App component.

```
import { createContext, Dispatch, SetStateAction, useContext, useState } from 'react';

const ThemeContext = createContext<string | undefined>('dark');

type UserContextType = {
  user: string | null;
  setUser: Dispatch<SetStateAction<string | null>>;
};
const UserContext = createContext<UserContextType>({
  user: null,
```

261

```
  setUser: () => undefined,
});

const Greeting = () => {
  const { user } = useContext(UserContext);

  return <p>Welcome, {user}.</p>;
};

const LoginForm = () => {
  const { setUser } = useContext(UserContext);
  const [firstName, setFirstName] = useState<string>('');
  const [lastName, setLastName] = useState<string>('');
  const isValidUser = firstName !== '' && lastName !== '';

  const onClick = () => {
    setUser(`${firstName} ${lastName}`);
  };

  return (
    <>
      <label>
        First Name:
        <input
          required
          value={firstName}
          onChange={(e) => setFirstName(e.target.value)}
        />
      </label>
      <label>
        Last Name:
        <input
          required
          value={lastName}
          onChange={(e) => setLastName(e.target.value)}
        />
      </label>
      <button type="button" disabled={!isValidUser} onClick={onClick}>
        Log In
      </button>
      {!isValidUser && <p>First and Last Name are required.</p>}
    </>
  );
};

const Panel = () => {
  const { user } = useContext(UserContext);

  const result = user ? <Greeting /> : <LoginForm />;
```

```
    return <div>{result}</div>;
};

const App = () => {
  const [theme, setTheme] = useState<string>('light');
  const [user, setUser] = useState<string | null>(null);

  const changeTheme = () => {
    setTheme((theme) => (theme === 'light' ? 'dark' : 'light'));
  };

  return (
    <ThemeContext.Provider value={theme}>
      <button onClick={changeTheme}>Change Theme</button>
      <UserContext.Provider
        value={{
          user,
          setUser,
        }}
      >
        <Panel />
      </UserContext.Provider>
      <p>Theme: {theme}</p>
    </ThemeContext.Provider>
  );
};

export { App };
```

To create the `UserContext` with the `createContext` function, we defined a TypeScript type for `UserContext`, and called it `UserContextType`. This type defines a `user` variable and a `setUser` updater method.

The `user` variable can either be a `string` or `null`. The `setUser` updater method's type matches the `user` variable, being defined as a `Dispatch` of type `SetStateAction<string | null>`. The `user` in `UserContext` is initialized with a value of `null`.

The value of `UserContext.Provider` is set using a `{ user, setUser }` object, with the `user` state variable and `setUser` state setter function coming from the `useState` Hook.

The `ThemeContext` is a simpler context, using `useState` to manage a string representation of the current theme. The theme is initialized with a value of "dark".

In the App component, nested within the `ThemeContext.Provider` is the `UserContext.Provider`, which only wraps the `Panel` component. This makes the theme state

263

available across the component tree, but the user state is only available within the `Panel` component and it's children (`Greeting` and `LoginForm`).

The `Panel` component uses the `useContext` Hook to read the `user` from the `UserContext`. Then, it checks if a current user has been set. If so, it renders a `Greeting` component. If not, it renders a `LoginForm` so that the current user can log in.

The `Greeting` component uses the `useContext` Hook to read the `user` from the `UserContext`. Then, it displays a greeting for the logged in user.

The `LoginForm` component uses the `useContext` Hook to access the `setUser` function from `UserContext`. It uses `setUser` to set the name of the user that logs in. Once the user is logged in, the `Greeting` component is displayed.

Extracting providers to a component

We can group context providers into a dedicated React component. Large React applications usually end up using several different contexts at the root level of the application. Grouping these contexts into a single React component makes the code cleaner and more maintainable.

This next example will make use of the previous example on multiple contexts. The main change in this example will be that a `MyContextProviders` component will encapsulate (hide) the internal context details of both the `ThemeContext` and the `UserContext`. The `MyContextProviders` component will then render the `children` passed to it within its context providers.

```
import { createContext, Dispatch, ReactNode, SetStateAction, useContext, useState } from 'react';

type ThemeContextType = {
  theme: string;
  changeTheme: () => void;
};
const ThemeContext = createContext<ThemeContextType>({
  theme: 'dark',
  changeTheme: () => undefined,
});

type UserContextType = {
  user: string | null;
  setUser: Dispatch<SetStateAction<string | null>>;
};
```

```typescript
const UserContext = createContext<UserContextType>({
  user: null,
  setUser: () => undefined,
});

type Props = {
  children: ReactNode;
};

const MyContextProviders = ({ children }: Props) => {
  const [user, setUser] = useState<string | null>(null);
  const [theme, setTheme] = useState<string>('dark');

  const changeTheme = () => {
    setTheme((theme) => (theme === 'light' ? 'dark' : 'light'));
  };

  return (
    <ThemeContext.Provider
      value={{
        theme,
        changeTheme,
      }}
    >
      <UserContext.Provider
        value={{
          user,
          setUser,
        }}
      >
        {children}
      </UserContext.Provider>
      <p>Theme: {theme}</p>
    </ThemeContext.Provider>
  );
};

const ThemeSwitcher = () => {
  const { changeTheme } = useContext(ThemeContext);

  return <button onClick={changeTheme}>Change Theme</button>;
};

const Greeting = () => {
  const { user } = useContext(UserContext);

  return <p>Welcome, {user}.</p>;
};

const LoginForm = () => {
```

```
  const { setUser } = useContext(UserContext);
  const [firstName, setFirstName] = useState<string>('');
  const [lastName, setLastName] = useState<string>('');
  const isValidUser = firstName !== '' && lastName !== '';

  const onClick = () => {
    setUser(`${firstName} ${lastName}`);
  };

  return (
    <>
      <label>
        First Name:
        <input
          required
          value={firstName}
          onChange={(e) => setFirstName(e.target.value)}
        />
      </label>
      <label>
        Last Name:
        <input
          required
          value={lastName}
          onChange={(e) => setLastName(e.target.value)}
        />
      </label>
      <button type="button" disabled={!isValidUser} onClick={onClick}>
        Log In
      </button>
      {!isValidUser && <p>First and Last Name are required.</p>}
    </>
  );
};

const Panel = () => {
  const { user } = useContext(UserContext);

  const result = user ? <Greeting /> : <LoginForm />;

  return <div>{result}</div>;
};

const App = () => {
  return (
    <MyContextProviders>
      <ThemeSwitcher />
      <Panel />
    </MyContextProviders>
  );
```

```
};
export { App };
```

The App and the ThemeSwitcher components are the only ones that changed when compared to the previous for using multiple contexts. The new component introduced for this example is MyContextProviders.

When multiple contexts are needed at the same level of the component tree, moving them to a dedicated component like MyContextProviders is a good idea. In the example above, that level is the the App component level, which is also the root level.

The MyContextProviders component defines providers for the ThemeContext and the UserContext. Rather than defining each context provider separately, we centralized them into one component, the MyContextProviders component. This way, we only need to consult one component when we need to make changes to the context providers.

We centralized the context state logic for the theme and the user in the MyContextProviders component. For organization purposes, this is better than leaving it in the App component. The theme and user state variables, as well as their corresponding state setter functions, are passed to each respective context provider.

Notice that we moved the "Change Theme" button to a dedicated component called ThemeSwitcher, which is nested in the component tree of MyContextProviders. This allows the ThemeSwitcher component to use the state of ThemeContext in order to update the theme.

The App component can no longer update the state of ThemeContext because the App component is not nested within the component tree of MyContextProviders. Thus, all theme-related state logic was moved out of the App component and into the MyContextProviders component.

Combining context with a reducer

Reducers help us organize state update logic, and context helps us pass information deep down to other components without props. This makes using them together a great combination!

Context is usually combined with a reducer to manage complex state logic. This approach is especially useful in large React applications. We can extract the state logic out of component files and move it to a file that contains the reducer and the context.

To combine a reducer with context, we will:

1. Create the reducer.
2. Create the context.
3. Use the context in the component tree.

For this next example, we will create a context and a reducer to manage product listings and make the state of products accessible across the component tree.

We will create a separate `ProductsContext.tsx` file that will hold both the reducer and the context. This will keep our React components clean and uncluttered, focused simply on displaying data.

1. Create the reducer

After creating the `ProductsContext.tsx` file, we'll define a `productsReducer` function in it, as well as the types and initial state required for the reducer. The reducer manages the state of products, allowing us to read products from the list, as well as add, edit, and delete products from the list.

```
import { createContext, ReactNode, useContext, useReducer } from 'react';

type Product = {
  id: number;
  name: string;
}

type ProductsState = {
  products: Product[];
}

enum ProductActionType {
  AddProduct = 'ADD_PRODUCT',
  EditProduct = 'EDIT_PRODUCT',
  DeleteProduct = 'DELETE_PRODUCT',
}

type ProductAction =
  | { type: ProductActionType.AddProduct; payload: Product }
  | { type: ProductActionType.EditProduct; payload: Product }
  | { type: ProductActionType.DeleteProduct; payload: number };

const initialState: ProductsState = {
  products: [
    { id: 1, name: "Nintendo Switch" },
```

```
    { id: 2, name: "Sony PlayStation" },
    { id: 3, name: "XBOX Series X" },
  ],
};

const productsReducer = (state: ProductsState, action: ProductAction): Produc
tsState => {
  const { type, payload } = action;

  switch (type) {
    case ProductActionType.AddProduct: {
      return {
        ...state,
        products: [...state.products, payload],
      };
    }
    case ProductActionType.EditProduct: {
      const updatedProducts = state.products.map((product) =>
        product.id === payload.id ? payload : product
      );
      return { products: updatedProducts };
    }
    case ProductActionType.DeleteProduct: {
      const filteredProducts = state.products.filter(
        (product) => product.id !== payload
      );
      return { products: filteredProducts };
    }
    default: {
      return state;
    }
  }
}
```

2. Create the context

Continuing in the `ProductsContext.tsx` file, we will now define the `ProductsContext`, a `ProductsProvider` component, and a `useProductsContext` custom Hook. The custom Hook will allow us to use the products context within components.

We'll use TypeScript to define the type for our `ProductsContext`. The `value` for the `ProductsProvider` will be composed of the reducer's state and dispatch function.

```
type ProductsDispatch = (action: ProductAction) => void;
type ProductsContextType = {
  state: ProductsState;
  dispatch: ProductsDispatch;
```

```
};

const ProductsContext = createContext<ProductsContextType | undefined>(undefi
ned);

type Props = {
  children: ReactNode;
}

const ProductsProvider = ({ children }: Props) => {
  const [state, dispatch] = useReducer(
    productsReducer,
    initialState,
  );

  return (
    <ProductsContext.Provider value={{ state, dispatch }}>
      {children}
    </ProductsContext.Provider>
  );
}

const useProductsContext = () => {
  const context = useContext(ProductsContext);
  if (context === undefined) {
    throw new Error("useProductsContext must be used within a ProductsProvide
r");
  }
  return context;
}

export type { Product }
export { ProductActionType, ProductsProvider, useProductsContext }
```

The ProductsProvider encapsulates the products context provider in a dedicated React component. It makes use of the useReducer Hook to get the state and dispatch for the products state. Both are then composed into an object and passed as the context value for the products context provider.

Within the useProductsContext custom Hook, we added a validation check for cases where context is undefined. If this occurs, the component that is trying to use this custom Hook is likely not wrapped with the provider of the products context, defined in the ProductsProvider component. The undefined value comes from the fact that we initialized the ProductsContext with undefined when we created it.

3. Use the context in the component tree

We'll now create a `ProductsApp.tsx` file. The `ProductsApp` component will wrap its component tree with the `ProductsProvider` component, making the state of the `ProductsContext` accessible across the component tree.

Wrapped within the `ProductsProvider` will be an `AddProduct` component and a `ProductsList` component. These components will make use of the `useProductsContext` custom Hook in order to read from state and modify the state of the `ProductsContext`.

```
import { AddProduct } from './AddProduct';
import { ProductsList } from './ProductsList';
import { ProductsProvider } from './ProductsContext';

const ProductsApp = () => {
  return (
    <ProductsProvider>
      <h4>Products</h4>
      <AddProduct />
      <ProductsList />
    </ProductsProvider>
  );
};

export { ProductsApp };
```

Let's take a look at the `ProductsList` component.

```
import { Product, ProductActionType, useProductsContext } from './ProductsContext';

const ProductsList = () => {
  const { state, dispatch } = useProductsContext();
  const { products } = state;

  const editProduct = (product: Product) => {
    dispatch({ type: ProductActionType.EditProduct, payload: product });
  };

  const deleteProduct = (id: number) => {
    dispatch({ type: ProductActionType.DeleteProduct, payload: id });
  };

  return (
    <ul>
      {products.map(({ id, name }) => (
```

271

```
      <li key={id}>
        <input
          value={name}
          onChange={(e) =>
            editProduct({ id, name: e.target.value })
          }
        />
        <button onClick={() => deleteProduct(id)}>Delete</button>
      </li>
    ))}
  </ul>
 );
};

export { ProductsList };
```

The ProductsList component references the ProductsContext via the useProductsContext custom Hook. It reads products from the context's state in order to display a list of products. It also dispatches product edit and delete actions to that same state via the dispatch function.

Lastly, let's take a look at the AddProduct component.

```
import { useState } from 'react';
import { ProductActionType, useProductsContext } from './ProductsContext';

const AddProduct = () => {
  const [productName, setProductName] = useState<string>('');
  const { state, dispatch } = useProductsContext();

  const addProduct = () => {
    if (productName.length) {
      dispatch({
        type: ProductActionType.AddProduct,
        payload: {
          id: Math.max(...state.products.map((item) => item.id)) + 1,
          name: productName,
        },
      });
      setProductName('');
    }
  };

  return (
    <>
      <input
        placeholder="Add new product"
        value={productName}
```

```
        onChange={e => setProductName(e.target.value)}
      />
      <button onClick={addProduct}>Add Product</button>
    </>
  );
};

export { AddProduct };
```

Just like the `ProductsList` component, the `AddProduct` component also references the `ProductsContext` via the `useProductsContext` custom Hook.

When the "Add Product" button is clicked, the `addProduct` event handler checks if a product name was entered in the text input. If so, it dispatches a product creation action to the context's state in order to add the new product. The `productName` state variable in `AddProduct` is then reset to an empty string so that we can add more products using the text input.

In order to construct the payload of the `dispatch` within the `addProduct` event handler, the list of products is read from the context's state. This is done in order to compute an `id` for the newly added product. The newly submitted `productName` is also added to the payload.

Before going with context

Sharing state between React components is a common challenge. Before going with context, we should consider lifting state up to the closest common parent component. However, a side effect of lifting state is that it may cause prop drilling.

When we find ourselves in a prop drilling situation where we are passing props a few levels deep, context is not the only solution to choose from. Before using context to solve prop drilling, we should consider using component composition via the special `children` prop. The `children` prop makes it easy to compose and combine React components.

So, how does component composition help us with passing props down many levels? We'll find out how in an example below. First, we'll look at an example of prop drilling. Then, we'll see how context can solve the prop drilling. Lastly, we'll compare the context solution with a component composition solution to see which solution is better at solving the prop drilling.

Prop drilling

Let's take a look at the following example of prop drilling. It consists of a main App component that displays a Dashboard for logged in users. The Dashboard receives a currentUser prop that it doesn't use directly. Instead, it just passes the currentUser prop along to its child components. This creates prop drilling.

```
import { useState } from "react";

type User = {
  name: string;
};

const App = () => {
  // global state that is usually put into context
  const [currentUser, setCurrentUser] = useState<User>();

  return (
    <div style={{ display: "flex", flexDirection: "column" }}>
      <div style={{ background: "lightgray" }}>
        <Header />
      </div>
      <div>
       {currentUser ? (
          <Dashboard user={currentUser} />
        ) : (
          <Login onLogin={() => setCurrentUser({ name: "John" })} />
        )}
      </div>
      <div style={{ background: "lightgray" }}>
        <Footer />
      </div>
    </div>
  )
}

export { App };

const Header = () => {
  return (
    <div>
      <h1>Header</h1>
    </div>
  )
}

const Footer = () => {
```

```
    return (
      <div>
        <h1>Footer</h1>
      </div>
    )
}

const Login = ({ onLogin }: { onLogin: () => void }) => {
    return (
      <div>
        <h2>Login</h2>
        <button onClick={onLogin}>Login</button>
      </div>
    )
}

const Dashboard = ({ user }: { user: User }) => {
    return (
     <div>
        <h2>Dashboard</h2>
        <DashboardNavigation />
        <DashboardContent user={user} />
      </div>
    )
}

const DashboardNavigation = () => {
    return (
      <div>
        <h3>Dashboard Navigation</h3>
      </div>
    )
}

const DashboardContent = ({ user }: { user: User }) => {
    return (
      <div>
        <h3>Dashboard Content</h3>
        <WelcomeMessage user={user} />
      </div>
    )
}

const WelcomeMessage = ({ user }: { user: User }) => {
    return (
      <div>
        <p>Welcome, {user.name}.</p>
      </div>
    )
}
```

The `Dashboard` and `DashboardContent` components receive a `user` prop, but both components don't actually use it. They just forward the `user` prop to the `WelcomeMessage` component. The first component in the component hierarchy that actually reads the `user` data is the `WelcomeMessage` component. At this level in the component hierarchy, we are nested several levels deep. The `currentUser` state that is declared in the `App` component does not get used until it is passed four levels deep into the `WelcomeMessage` component.

Solving prop drilling with context

We can solve the prop drilling of the `user` prop by putting the `currentUser` state into context. Then, we can retrieve the `currentUser` from that context in the `WelcomeMessage` component.

Let's create a `UserContext` and wrap the elements returned by the App component within a context provider. Then, we'll remove the `user` prop from the component hierarchy. Lastly, we'll use the `useContext` Hook in the `WelcomeMessage` component to retrieve the `currentUser` from the `UserContext`.

```
import { createContext, useContext, useState } from "react";

type User = {
  name: string;
};

type UserContextType = {
  currentUser: User | null;
};

const UserContext = createContext<UserContextType>({ currentUser: null });

const App = () => {
    const [currentUser, setCurrentUser] = useState<User | null>(null);

    return (
        <UserContext.Provider value={{ currentUser }}>
            <div style={{ display: "flex", flexDirection: "column" }}>
                <div style={{ background: "lightgray" }}>
                    <Header />
                </div>
                <div>
                    {currentUser ? (
                        <Dashboard />
                    ) : (
                        <Login onLogin={() => setCurrentUser({ name: "John" }
)} />
```

```
                    )}
                </div>
                <div style={{ background: "lightgray" }}>
                    <Footer />
                </div>
            </div>
        </UserContext.Provider>
    )
}

export { App };

// ...

const Dashboard = () => {
    return (
        <div>
            <h2>Dashboard</h2>
            <DashboardNavigation />
            <DashboardContent />
        </div>
    )
}

const DashboardContent = () => {
    return (
        <div>
            <h3>Dashboard Content</h3>
            <WelcomeMessage />
        </div>
    )
}

const WelcomeMessage = () => {
  const { currentUser } = useContext(UserContext);

    return (
        <div>
            <p>Welcome, {currentUser?.name}.</p>
        </div>
    )
}
```

Context fixes the prop drilling. There's no more drilling of props down multiple levels of components. The `Dashboard` and `DashboardContent` components have been simplified by removing their unnecessary `user` props. The `WelcomeMessage` now has direct access to the data that it needs.

The problem with this solution is that the `WelcomeMessage` component cannot be rendered outside of the context provider for `UserContext`. Rendering the `WelcomeMessage` outside of the context provider will cause `currentUser` to be `null`, leaving us unable to access the actual value for `currentUser` that the context provider makes available.

Another problem with this solution is that we need to check if the `currentUser` is defined in the `WelcomeMessage` component. We did this with JavaScript's optional chaining operator. However, if no `currentUser` is defined, we should not even be rendering the `WelcomeMessage` component. No welcome message is needed if no user is defined. It's assumed that we have a `currentUser` when we render the `WelcomeMessage` component, but that may not always be the case. We need more flexibility.

The complexity of context ends up trickling down the component hierarchy in the example above. This complexity can be avoided with component composition. Composition gives us the flexibility to be more explicit with our component usage.

Solving prop drilling with composition

The `Dashboard` component is quite general for a component. It's hard to know what's inside it. It can be used to render lots of different things. It could render navigation, a sidebar, a content area, a welcome message, and more.

In it's current state, `Dashboard` is not a composable component. We can't pick which elements we want to render as part of the dashboard. We want the `Dashboard` component to be composable so that we can assemble various combinations of components to be rendered by it. This will allow us to pass the `WelcomeMessage`, with the `user` prop set, directly into the `Dashboard` component. This will result in no more prop drilling.

The special `children` prop is the key to component composition. Let's start from the initial example that suffered from prop drilling. Let's remove the `user` prop from the component hierarchy. Then, let's add the special `children` prop to the `Dashboard` component and the `DashboardContent` component. This will eliminate two levels of prop drilling. Lastly, let's compose what we want the `Dashboard` component to render by including the desired elements within the `Dashboard` tags in the `App` component.

```
import { ReactNode, useState } from "react";

type User = {
  name: string;
};

const App = () => {
    const [currentUser, setCurrentUser] = useState<User | null>(null);

    return (
    <div style={{ display: "flex", flexDirection: "column" }}>
      <div style={{ background: "lightgray" }}>
        <Header />
      </div>
      <div>
        {currentUser ? (
          <Dashboard>
            <DashboardNavigation />
            <DashboardContent>
              <WelcomeMessage user={currentUser} />
            </DashboardContent>
          </Dashboard>
        ) : (
          <Login onLogin={() => setCurrentUser({ name: "John" })} />
        )}
      </div>
      <div style={{ background: "lightgray" }}>
        <Footer />
      </div>
    </div>
    )
}

export { App };

// ...

const Dashboard = ({ children }: { children: ReactNode }) => {
    return (
        <div>
            <h2>Dashboard</h2>
            {children}
        </div>
    )
}

// ...

const DashboardContent = ({ children }: { children: ReactNode }) => {
    return (
```

```
        <div>
            <h3>Dashboard Content</h3>
            {children}
        </div>
    )
}

const WelcomeMessage = ({ user }: { user: User }) => {
  return (
        <div>
            <p>Welcome, {user.name}.</p>
        </div>
    )
}
```

The Dashboard and DashboardContent components no longer need to receive a user prop. The only component receiving the user prop is the one that needs it, the WelcomeMessage component.

The prop drilling is fixed. This solution needed just one prop, thanks to component composition via the children prop. Using component composition to solve prop drilling is often simpler than using context.

The children prop provides us with the flexibility to compose our dashboard in any way that we want. We can remove the DashboardNavigation, or we can choose to include it. We get to choose what is rendered by the Dashboard component.

When it comes to solving prop drilling, consider component composition before resorting to using context.

Recap

- Avoid putting all your data and state into context just because you want to access it from anywhere.
- React context is meant for data that does not need to be updated often.
- Context is best used for data that really needs to be kept global, such as theme, language, and user settings.
- Before implementing context to solve prop drilling, consider component composition instead.
- Context lets a parent component provide data to the entire tree below it - without using props.
- We can override context for a specific part of the component tree.
- We can use multiple independent contexts in a React application.
- Splitting up contexts by responsibility is better than using one large context.
- A reducer can be combined with context to manage more complex state.
- Components can be decluttered by moving context and reducer code to one file.
- A React application can consist of many context-reducer pairs.

What's next?

Congratulations on completing this book! You've gained a solid understanding of how to build modern web applications with React and TypeScript.

Throughout this book, we've explored the core concepts of React. React is a powerful and flexible library for building interactive user interfaces. With its component-based architecture, declarative syntax, and efficient rendering model, there is no limit to what we can build with React.

By mastering the fundamentals covered in this book, you will be well equipped to continue learning and building with React for years to come.

I hope you enjoyed your journey through this book. As you've seen, React makes it fun and easy to create web applications. I encourage you to keep having fun with what you learned by building an awesome website or web application with React!

I invite you to visit my website (https://lumin8media.com) for more JavaScript, TypeScript, and React content to help you continue your learning journey.

Lastly, I will leave you with a few topics that I recommend exploring in order to continue your learning journey with React. These topics are *routing, complex state,* and using a *React framework.* Covering these large topics went beyond the scope of this book. Each of these topics would merit its own dedicated book. Check out the links provided below to start diving into these topics.

Routing

React Router (https://reactrouter.com) is a third-party library for routing in React applications. It's the best way to build a navigation system so that we can navigate to different pages in a React application.

No matter what type of website or web application you're building, React Router will help you keep your routing logic simple.

My other book, **React Router Ready: Learn React Router with React and TypeScript** (https://lumin8media.com/books/react-router-ready-learn-react-router-with-react-and-typescript), will teach you everything you need to know about React Router to start building effective React apps. The book is project-based, which means that you'll learn all the React Router fundamentals while having fun building a realistic project.

Complex state

If your React application is complex and requires managing large, complex state that must to be shared across many components, consider an advanced state management tool like **Redux** (https://redux.js.org). Redux is a third-party library for managing global state. Redux provides a centralized store for managing global state in a React application.

Zustand (https://github.com/pmndrs/zustand) is a newer state management library that is simpler to use than Redux. It uses a similar approach to Redux, but with a more lightweight API. It's worth checking out, especially if you find Redux a bit too overwhelming for your needs.

A React framework

Next.js (Next.js) is a React framework that provides all the building blocks needed to build modern web apps with React. As a framework, Next.js takes care of all the tooling and configuration needed for React projects. Next.js offers an organized project structure, performance optimizations, and features such as routing, data fetching, server-side rendering, and several integrations.

Next.js provides a great experience for developers and end-users alike. Once you get more comfortable with React, I recommend looking into Next.js. A good way to get started with this framework is to start using it to build a small React side project.

Printed in Great Britain
by Amazon